Copy Editor & Interior Design: Constance Santego
Book Layout: ©2017 BookDesignTemplates.com

Ordering Information:
Quantity sales. Special discounts are available on quantity purchases by corporations, associations, and others. For details, contact the "Special Sales Department" at the address above.

Trade Paperback ISBN: 978-1-990062-96-4
Ebook ISBN 978-1-990062-97-1
Created and published In Canada. Printed and bound in the United States of America

First Edition
Published by Maximillian Enterprises
Kelowna, BC Canada
www.constancesantego.ca

Sacral Chakra 101: Creativity, Pleasure, Emotions

"Balance Your Emotions, Ignite Your Creativity, Reclaim Your Joy"

(Vol III)

Dr. Constance Santego

Maximillian Enterprises
Kelowna, BC

Dedication

To the flow of life itself —
the waters of emotion, creativity, and connection that move
through us all.

May this book remind you that your feelings are sacred, your
creativity divine, and your pleasure a birthright.
May you dance again with your inner rhythm,
honor your emotions as teachers,
and rediscover the joy of being fully, vibrantly alive.

— Dr. Constance Santego

ALSO BY DR. CONSTANCE SANTEGO

NOVELS
Illegitimate Grace
Ashcroft Hollow

Okanagan Trilogy:
Beneath the Vineyards
Under the Okanagan Sun
Guardian of the Lake

The Nine Spiritual Gifts Series:
Journey of a Soul – (Vol 1 Michael)
Language of a Soul – (Vol 2 Gabriel)
Prophecy of a Soul – (Vol 3 Bath Kol)
Healing of a Soul – (Vol 4 Raphael)
Miracles of a Soul – (Vol 5 Hamied)
Knowledge of a Soul – (Vol 6 Raziel)
Wisdom of a Soul – (Vol 7 Uriel)
Faith of a Soul – (Vol 8 Pistis Sophia)

NONFICTION
The Intuitive Life, The Gift Of Prophecy, Third Edition
Fairy Tales, Dreams And Reality… Where Are You On Your Path? Second Edition
Your Persona… The Mask You Wear
Archangel Michael's Soul Retrieval Guide
Tesla And The Future Of Energy Medicine
Beyond Tesla: Advancing The Science Of Energy Healing
Tesla's Code: Mastering Energy, Frequency, And Creative Power
Beyond The Mind: Harnessing The Power Of Astral Projection For Creative Awakening
Bend, Don't Break: Finding Your Way Back To Abundance
Ring Therapy: A Guide To Healing And Balance
Ring Therapy Pocket Guide
Floraopathy™: The Art And Science Of Vibrational Healing With Essential Oils
Dear Older Me: A Memoir… Of Sorts
It's Just Like Poker: A Spiritual Guide To Playing The Cards Life Deals You
Signs And Meanings: What The Feet Reveal About Health, Stress, And The Body's Story
Auricions: Unlocking Subconscious Healing Through Quantum Medicine
Quick Fix Acupressure Method
Manifestation – The DREAM Method in 5 Steps
Confidence- Mastering the Dream Method

REIKI WISDOM, SERIES:
Angelic Lifestyle, a Vibrant Lifestyle
Angelic Lifestyle 42-Day Energy Cleanse
Reiki and the Power of The Joint Points: Unlocking Energy Pathways for Healing (Vol I)
Reiki and Karmic Healing: Releasing Patterns From Past Lives (Vol II)
Reiki and the Five Elements (Vol III)
Secrets of a Healer, Magic Of Reiki
The Reiki Master's Manual

CHAKRA SERIES:
Heart Chakra 101: The Bridge
Root Chakra 101: Building Safety, Survival, Foundation
Sacral Chakra 101: Creativity, Pleasure, Emotions
Solar Plexus Chakra 101: Power, Confidence, Will
Throat Chakra 101: Truth, Voice, Self-Expression
Third Eye Chakra 10: Intuition, Vision, Insight
Crown Chakra 10: Spiritual Connection, Transcendence.

SECRETS OF A HEALER, SERIES:
Magic Of Aromatherapy (Vol I)
Magic Of Reflexology (Vol II)
Magic Of The Gifts (Vol III)
Magic Of Muscle Testing (Vol IV)
Magic Of Iridology (Vol V)
Magic Of Massage (Vol VI)
Magic Of Hypnotherapy (Vol VII)
Magic Of Reiki (Vol VIII)
Magic Of Advanced Aromatherapy (Vol IX)
Magic Of Esthetics (Vol X)
The Reiki Master's Manual (Vol XI)

ADULT COLORING JOURNALS
SERIES-ZEN COLORING:
Quantum Energy and Mindful Living Journal (Vol 1)
Reiki Energy Journal (Vol 2)
Nine Spiritual Gifts Journal (Vol 3)
I Forgive Journal (Vol 4)

FOR CHILDREN
I am Big Tonight. I Don't Need the Light
The Magic Elf Book: 25 Days of Surprises

COOKBOOK
My Favorite Recipes, with a Hint of Giggle

BUISNESS
How To Use ChatGPT For Authors: From Idea To Published Book
Scaling Beyond 6 Figures: Strategies For Health & Wellness Professionals
The Academypreneur's Playbook: Turn Knowledge Into A
Revenue-Generating School

HUMOR/GIFT BOOK
How Do You Like Your Eggs? Crack Into Your Personality, Yolk and All

Contents

Preface

Introduction: Returning to the Flow of Being

When we began our journey with the **Heart Chakra**, we stepped into the center of the human energy system — the bridge between body and spirit, earth and sky, self and other. The heart teaches us compassion, connection, and the power of love. Yet even love needs both a foundation beneath it and a channel through which it can be expressed.

This is why we next turned to the **Root Chakra**, or *Muladhara*. Located at the base of the spine, it is the ground of our being — the place of safety, survival, and belonging. The root anchors us to the earth, giving us stability and strength. Without this ground, even the most open heart may falter, for love cannot blossom where fear, insecurity, or instability persist.

And yet, safety and survival are not the whole story of being human. Once the roots are strong, life calls us to feel, to create, to relate. This is where the **Sacral Chakra**, or *Svadhisthana*, enters the journey. Situated just below the navel, it governs our emotions, creativity, intimacy, and sensuality. Where the root gives us the right to exist, the sacral gives us permission to *experience* — to flow with life like water, to dance with desire, and to express the richness of who we are.

The body mirrors this progression. The root grounds us through the legs, bones, and muscles, while the sacral animates the hips, pelvis, reproductive system, and the waters of the body. It is the tide of emotions, the spark of inspiration, the rhythm of creation. When Svadhisthana is balanced, we feel alive, inspired, and emotionally free. When imbalanced, repression, shame, or addiction can either dry us up or sweep us away.

In this way, heart, root, and sacral form a vital triad. The **heart opens us to love**, the **root steadies that love on solid ground**, and the **sacral allows love to flow into creativity, intimacy, and joy**. Just as a tree can only stretch toward the sky if its roots are firm and its sap flows freely, so too our spiritual awakening depends on both grounding and flow.

This book is an invitation to explore that flow. Together, we will uncover the wisdom of the Sacral Chakra: its symbols and stories, its shadows and gifts, and its practical tools for healing and balance. Through reflection, creative expression, and practices that honor the waters within, you will learn how to restore your flow of being — and from that flow, rise into life with passion, pleasure, and emotional freedom.

About the Chakra 101 Series

The *Chakra 101* series is a journey through the seven primary energy centers of the human body — a guided exploration of how spirit expresses itself through matter, and how healing unfolds layer by layer. Each book in this series blends ancient wisdom with modern energy practices, bridging spirituality, psychology, and embodiment to help readers rediscover balance and wholeness.

The series began with **Heart Chakra 101: The Bridge**, where love and compassion opened the way for inner transformation. From there, **Root Chakra 101: Building Safety, Survival, Foundation** grounded that love into the physical world, teaching stability, trust, and the sacredness of belonging. Now, in **Sacral Chakra 101: Creativity, Pleasure, Emotions**, the journey flows forward — from stability to movement, from survival to creation, from love as an ideal to love as an experience felt through the body.

Each book in this series builds upon the last, guiding you upward through the chakra system:

1. **Heart Chakra 101** – The Bridge of Love and Compassion
2. **Root Chakra 101** – Building Safety, Survival, Foundation
3. **Sacral Chakra 101** – Creativity, Pleasure, Emotions
4. **Solar Plexus Chakra 101** – Power, Confidence, and Will
5. **Throat Chakra 101** – Expression, Authenticity, and Truth
6. **Third Eye Chakra 101** – Intuition, Vision, and Clarity
7. **Crown Chakra 101** – Spirit, Consciousness, and Unity

While each volume stands on its own, together they form a complete map — a journey from earth to sky, from the physical to the divine. This path through the chakras mirrors the journey of awakening itself: beginning with love, rooting into safety, awakening creative flow, discovering purpose, speaking truth, seeing clearly, and ultimately remembering our oneness with all that is.

Whether you are a student of energy medicine, a healer, or a seeker of self-understanding, the *Chakra 101* series is designed to guide you home — to your body, your energy, and your divine essence.

Chapter 1 – Entering the Flow of Being

The Role of the Sacral Chakra in the Chakra System

Every journey of energy unfolds step by step, and after finding our foundation in the Root Chakra, the next step rises into the **Sacral Chakra, Svadhisthana**. Though this series began at the heart — the bridge of love and balance — it is here, in the waters of the lower abdomen, that energy begins to move, flow, and create.

If the Root Chakra whispers, *"You are safe; you belong,"* the Sacral Chakra responds, *"Now you may feel; now you may create."* Where Muladhara gives us the ground to stand upon, Svadhisthana invites us into the dance of life. It governs our emotions, creativity, sensuality, and intimacy — the sacred right to experience pleasure, to express ourselves, and to connect with others not only for survival, but for joy.

The Sacral Chakra is associated with the **element of water**, ever-shifting and adaptive. Its color is vibrant orange — the glow of sunsets, ripe fruit, and living fire softened by fluidity. Its symbol, the six-petaled lotus with a crescent moon, reminds us of cycles: the ebb and flow of tides, emotions, and creativity. Just as the moon governs the waters of the earth, so too does this chakra govern the waters within us.

In the chakra system, Svadhisthana builds directly upon Muladhara. Without the grounding of the Root, the sacral cannot flow freely; fear and insecurity at the base will constrict the joy of emotional and creative expression. Yet when the Root is steady, the Sacral blossoms into vitality — passion arises, creativity awakens, and intimacy becomes safe and nourishing.

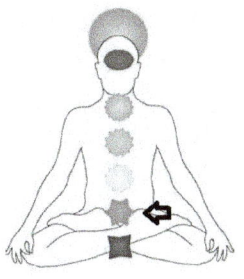

Think of Svadhisthana as the waters that rise once the roots of a tree have found soil. The tree may be anchored by the earth, but it lives through the sap that flows upward, carrying nourishment, vitality, and life-force to every branch. So too with us: our emotions, creativity, and desires are the living waters that allow our soul to flourish.

Svadhisthana is both the **second step** and the **river that carries us forward**. It is here we learn that being alive is more than existing — it is feeling, expressing, and creating. It is here that we reclaim the innocence of pleasure and the courage to flow with our emotions. Balanced, this chakra offers joy, adaptability, intimacy, and creative fire. Imbalanced, it may leave us numb, repressed, or swept away by excess.

In this way, Svadhisthana is not only the birthplace of creativity but also the bridge to higher evolution. From the Root, energy rises into the Sacral; from the Sacral, it flows into the Solar Plexus, where desire becomes will, and from there into the Heart, where passion transforms into love. Each center builds upon the other, and Svadhisthana ensures that the journey is not dry or mechanical but alive with the fullness of human experience.

The Sacral Chakra is an invitation: to feel deeply, to create boldly, and to flow freely. It reminds us that spiritual growth is not about denying desire but sanctifying it — allowing the waters of life to carry us closer to balance, wholeness, and awakening.

TRADITIONAL SANSKRIT NAMES

- **Svādhiṣṭhāna** (स्वाधिष्ठान) – most common Sanskrit name, meaning *"one's own abode"* or *"dwelling place of the self."*

COMMON ENGLISH NAMES

- **Sacral Chakra** – modern Western usage, referring to its location near the sacrum.
- **Spleen Chakra** – early Western esoteric writers (such as **C.W. Leadbeater** and the Theosophical Society in the late 1800s and early 1900s)
- **Second Chakra** – its position in the seven chakra system.
- **Creative Center** – linked to artistic, sexual, and emotional creativity.
- **Sex Chakra** (informal) – emphasizing its connection to sexuality and intimacy.
- **Seat of Emotions** – because it governs feelings, desire, and fluidity.

ELEMENTAL & SYMBOLIC ASSOCIATIONS

- **Water Chakra** – tied to the water element, flow, adaptability, and cleansing.
- **Moon Center** – linked to lunar cycles and rhythms (especially in Tantra).
- **Orange Chakra** – from its associated color in modern chakra systems.
- **Lotus of Six Petals** – referring to its symbol in traditional yogic texts.

CULTURAL / ESOTERIC NAMES

- **Shakti Chakra** – seat of feminine creative energy (Shakti).
- **Hara Center** (Japanese martial and healing traditions) – a point of power located below the navel, very close to the sacral chakra.
- **Dantian (Lower Field of Elixir)** (Taoist/Chinese Qi practices) – energy center in the same region, governing vitality and life force.
- **Pelvic Chakra** – anatomical reference in modern energy healing.

METAPHORICAL NAMES

- **Chakra of Desire** – seat of longing, pleasure, and intimacy.
- **Chakra of Flow** – representing movement, adaptability, and fluidity.
- **Womb of Creation** – symbolic of birthing ideas, art, and life itself.

Svadhisthana: The Flow of Human Experience

The Sanskrit name for the Sacral Chakra is **Svadhisthana**, a word filled with meaning. *Sva* translates to "self," and *adhisthana* means "dwelling place" or "seat." Together they reveal the essence of this chakra: the sacred dwelling place of the self — the inner home where feeling, creativity, and pleasure reside.

From the moment we leave the safety of the womb, our lives depend not only on survival but also on connection, comfort, and expression. The instincts of Muladhara give us the right to exist, but Svadhisthana grants us the right to *experience*. Eating not only nourishes but also brings taste. Breathing is not only survival but rhythm. Touch is not only sensation but intimacy. Just as water gives life to a seed once it is rooted in soil, the Sacral Chakra awakens vitality once grounding has been established.

Svadhisthana represents the emotional wisdom of the body. It is the part of us that longs for pleasure, that moves with desire, that dreams and creates. It teaches us that feeling is not a weakness, but a flow, and that creativity is not a luxury, but a necessity. Often overshadowed by the call to discipline or reason, this chakra reminds us that life without feeling becomes dry, and spirituality without joy becomes hollow.

When Svadhisthana is balanced, life feels vibrant and fluid. We allow ourselves to feel pleasure without guilt, to express creativity without fear, and to share intimacy with openness. Emotions flow like rivers — not stagnant, not overwhelming, but alive. When it is imbalanced, shame, repression, or addiction can bind us. We may feel cut off from joy, trapped in emotional storms, or disconnected from our bodies and desires. These imbalances ripple upward, dulling our confidence in the solar plexus, closing the heart to love, and clouding the mind's clarity.

In this way, Svadhisthana is not only the second chakra but the source of emotional and creative freedom. Without flow, the entire energetic system dries up; with flow, every other chakra can awaken with vibrancy and movement.

Just as a river carries nourishment unseen beneath its surface, your sacral chakra is the subtle current of life that keeps you inspired, expressive, and connected. It is here, in the orange waters of Svadhisthana, that your journey into pleasure, creativity, and emotional truth begins.

What Is Sanskrit and Why Does It Matter for Chakras?

The language most often associated with the chakras is **Sanskrit**, an ancient Indian language considered by many to be a *language of vibration*. Each chakra's name in Sanskrit not only identifies it but also embodies an energetic quality that reflects its essence.

For the **Sacral Chakra**, the Sanskrit name is **Svadhisthana**. *Sva* means "self," and *adhisthana* means "dwelling place" or "seat." Together, the word reveals this chakra as the *sacred home of the self* — the inner seat of emotions, creativity, and pleasure. Unlike a simple label, Sanskrit words are designed to be felt as much as spoken. Their sound vibration carries energy, influencing the body, mind, and subtle fields.

Sanskrit is significant for chakras because it preserves a system of sacred sound. Each chakra has a **bīja mantra** (seed sound) that resonates with its energy. For Svadhisthana, the sound is **VAM**. When spoken, sung, or chanted, "VAM" creates a fluid, flowing vibration that can be felt in the lower abdomen, activating the waters of creativity and emotional release. In this way, the sound itself becomes a healing tool, harmonizing the energy of the sacral chakra.

Sanskrit also provides a **symbolic framework**. The letters of the Sanskrit alphabet are often inscribed on the lotus petals of chakra mandalas, each sound linked to subtle qualities of energy. The six petals of Svadhisthana's lotus carry six Sanskrit syllables, each connected to aspects of desire, vitality, and emotional flow. Together, they remind us that language, vibration, and consciousness are inseparable.

Why does this matter today? Because **language shapes consciousness**. By engaging with the Sanskrit name, sound, and symbolism of Svadhisthana, we align ourselves with thousands of years of wisdom that recognized the body as more than flesh and bone — it is a temple of vibration. Chanting or meditating with Sanskrit words is not about tradition for its own sake, but about entering into resonance with the energetic essence of being human.

When you chant **"VAM,"** you are not just repeating a sound. You are affirming: *I am allowed to feel. I am creative. I am in flow.*

The Sacral Chakra and Maslow's Hierarchy of Needs

In the 20th century, psychologist **Abraham Maslow** introduced his **Hierarchy of Needs**, a framework describing the stages of human motivation. At the base of his pyramid are physiological needs — food, water, sleep, shelter — followed by safety needs like protection and stability. Only when these are met can a person move upward toward belonging, intimacy, esteem, and ultimately self-actualization.

This modern psychological model beautifully mirrors the chakra system. Just as Maslow understood that survival and safety must be in place before deeper growth, the yogic tradition recognized that the **Root Chakra** provides grounding, and the **Sacral Chakra** awakens the capacity for relationship, pleasure, and creative flow. Without safety, intimacy becomes fragile. Without emotional freedom, higher awareness becomes restricted.

- **Root Chakra ↔ Physiological & Safety Needs**
  Survival, stability, and security are the foundation. Without them, no further growth is possible.

- **Sacral Chakra ↔ Belonging, Intimacy & Emotional Flow**
  Once basic safety is established, energy rises into Svadhisthana. Here, Maslow's third level — *love and belonging* — comes alive. This chakra governs our ability to form healthy relationships, embrace our sensuality, and explore creativity. Without this level, we may feel isolated, creatively blocked, or emotionally unfulfilled.
- **Solar Plexus ↔ Esteem & Personal Power**
  A strong sense of identity, confidence, and personal will flows from balanced emotional expression.
- **Heart Chakra ↔ Love & Compassion**
  True love requires not only safety and esteem, but the emotional openness of the sacral chakra — the willingness to feel, connect, and trust.
- **Throat Chakra ↔ Authentic Expression**
  When relationships are healthy and emotions flow, the voice can speak truth.
- **Third Eye ↔ Vision & Intuition**
  Higher insight unfolds when emotions no longer bind or distort perception.
- **Crown Chakra ↔ Self-Actualization & Transcendence**
  Maslow's highest level mirrors the spiritual union described in yoga: unity with the divine.

Seen in this way, the chakra system and Maslow's hierarchy are two parallel maps of the same human journey. One comes from ancient yogic philosophy, the other from modern psychology — yet both reveal that wholeness begins with security, blossoms through emotional connection, and eventually rises into love, wisdom, and transcendence.

Just as we cannot reach the heart without grounding in the root, we cannot fully embody joy, intimacy, or creativity without first opening the sacral chakra. It is the bridge from survival to belonging — the place where life begins to flow.

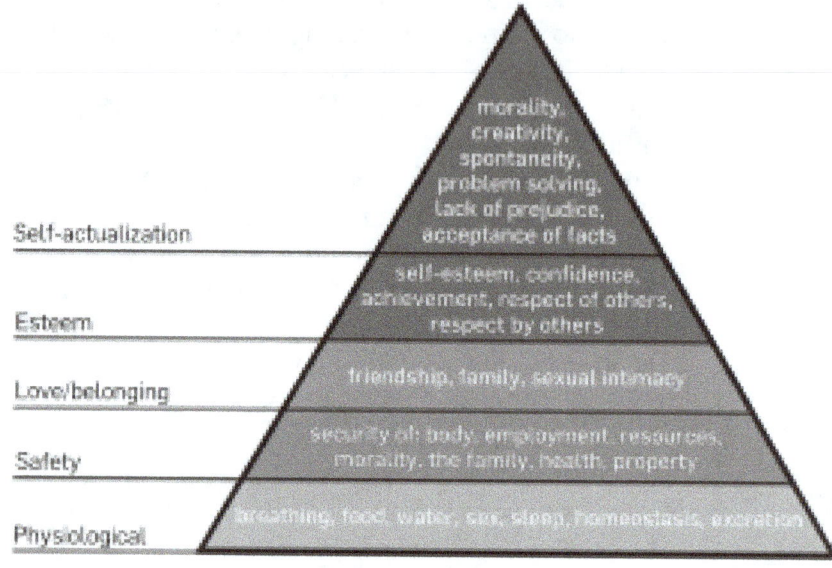

Mazlow's Hierarchy of Needs

Sacral Chakra ↔ Belonging, Intimacy & Emotional Flow

The Sacral Chakra (*Svadhisthana*) is the second energy center of the chakra system, just as *love and belonging* form the third level of Maslow's hierarchy. Once survival and safety are established through the Root Chakra, the human spirit naturally longs for connection, intimacy, and creative expression. Without flow at this level, the journey toward esteem, self-expression, and higher consciousness becomes blocked.

BELONGING NEEDS: THE HUMAN DESIRE TO CONNECT

At its heart, Svadhisthana governs our ability to form meaningful emotional and physical bonds. It teaches us that survival alone is not enough — life is meant to be shared.

- **Relationships:** Whether through family, friendships, or romantic partners, healthy relationships give us the sense of belonging that nourishes emotional well-being.
- **Intimacy:** Safe and consensual intimacy allows the body to experience pleasure and trust, strengthening the bridge between self and other.
- **Community:** Feeling part of a group, culture, or collective affirms that we are not alone, reinforcing the chakra's theme of shared flow.
- **Acceptance:** The freedom to be authentic without fear of rejection is a key marker of a balanced sacral chakra.

EMOTIONAL FLOW: THE WISDOM OF FEELING

Beyond external bonds, Svadhisthana is the home of our emotional body — the inner tides that rise and fall. It governs the ability to feel, release, and adapt.

- **Pleasure & Joy:** Permission to experience pleasure without guilt keeps the emotional body alive and responsive.
- **Creativity:** The sacral chakra is the wellspring of artistic and imaginative expression. When emotions are allowed to flow, creativity naturally follows.
- **Adaptability:** Like water, emotions must move. Suppression creates stagnation, while overindulgence floods the system. Balance is found in flow.
- **Emotional Intelligence:** Understanding and honoring our feelings — and the feelings of others — creates harmony in relationships.

WHY THIS MATTERS FOR ENERGY FLOW

Just as Maslow's hierarchy shows that unmet belonging needs lead to isolation and despair, the chakra system teaches that blocked sacral energy prevents higher development. If Svadhisthana is weak or unstable:

- The **Solar Plexus (Manipura)** may lack the emotional strength needed to develop confidence and willpower.
- The **Heart Chakra (Anahata)** may hesitate to open, for love requires trust in intimacy and the courage to feel.
- The **Throat Chakra (Vishuddha)** may struggle to express truth if emotions are repressed or unacknowledged.

When the Sacral Chakra is balanced, the entire system thrives. A flowing sacral center provides the inner affirmation: *"I am allowed to feel. I am allowed to connect. I am allowed to create."* With this assurance, energy rises toward empowerment, expression, and ultimately spiritual awakening.

Chapter 2 – Foundations of Muladhara

Sacral Chakra Basics: A Gentle Recap

If you are new to chakra study, the **Sacral Chakra**, or **Svadhisthana**, is the second of the seven main chakras. It is located in the lower abdomen, just below the navel, and extends into the pelvic region, hips, and reproductive organs. Where the Root Chakra grounds us into safety and survival, the Sacral Chakra invites us to flow — to feel, to create, and to connect with others through pleasure and intimacy.

The energy here is fluid and emotional. It governs our ability to enjoy life, embrace desire, and express creativity. Just as a river nourishes the land around it, Svadhisthana feeds the vitality of the entire energy system. Without flow at this level, the chakras above may feel dry, rigid, or disconnected.

Key qualities of Svadhisthana include:

- **Element:** Water — fluid, adaptable, cleansing, life-giving.
- **Color:** Vibrant orange — the hue of warmth, vitality, and creativity.
- **Symbol:** A six-petaled lotus containing a crescent moon within a circle, representing cycles, emotions, and the flowing tides of life.
- **Sound (Bija Mantra):** VAM — the seed syllable that resonates with the vibration of creativity, flow, and emotional release.

- **Location in the body:** Lower abdomen, pelvis, hips, reproductive organs, kidneys, and bladder.
- **Organs and systems:** Reproductive system, urinary tract, circulatory fluids, and hormonal balance (testes, ovaries).
- **Core themes:** Pleasure, creativity, sensuality, intimacy, emotional flow, adaptability, and relationship to self and others.

When Svadhisthana is **balanced**, you feel joyful, inspired, and emotionally free. Your creativity flows naturally, intimacy feels safe and nourishing, and you move through life with adaptability and passion.

When it is **blocked or weak**, you may feel emotionally numb, creatively stifled, or closed off from pleasure and intimacy. Shame, guilt, or repression often signal sacral imbalance.

When it is **overactive**, energy may be expressed as obsession, emotional overwhelm, or unhealthy attachments. Pleasure-seeking may become addictive, pulling you out of harmony rather than into flow.

Svadhisthana is the reminder that spirituality is not only about survival or transcendence but about embracing the beauty of life itself. By tending to the sacral chakra, you awaken your birthright to feel, create, and flow with the rhythm of being human. From this place, energy can rise into empowerment, love, and higher consciousness.

Cross-Cultural Perspectives on the Sacral

The concept of pleasure, creativity, and emotional flow is not unique to yoga or Sanskrit traditions. Across the world, cultures have recognized the importance of honoring the body's life force, cycles, and waters. Though the languages and symbols differ, the essence of **Svadhisthana** is universal: without flow, there can be no creation.

Yogic Tradition

In the yogic chakra system, Svadhisthana is the second chakra — the energy center of water, movement, and desire. It is symbolized by the six-petaled lotus, the crescent moon, and the sound **VAM**. Ancient yogis associated this chakra with sexuality, reproduction, and creativity — the waters that bring forth life. They taught that emotional energy, when honored, becomes the current that carries Kundalini upward. But when ignored or suppressed, these waters stagnate, preventing the natural rise of energy.

Shamanic Traditions

In many shamanic cultures, the sacral themes of water, emotion, and sensuality appear in rituals honoring rivers, lakes, and the cycles of the moon. Water is seen as a bridge between worlds — cleansing, nourishing, and carrying messages from spirit. Shamans often use drumming or dance to shift emotional energy, allowing the community to release grief, celebrate joy, or call in fertility. This mirrors Svadhisthana's role as the center of movement, passion, and emotional flow.

Indigenous Perspectives

Indigenous peoples around the world place deep importance on fertility, creativity, and the cycles of nature. The sacredness of menstruation, the honoring of childbirth, and the rituals surrounding planting and harvest are all expressions of sacral wisdom. Emotions are seen as currents that connect the individual to the tribe and to the rhythms of the earth. To repress feeling or disconnect from these cycles is viewed not only as a personal imbalance but also as a loss of harmony with the community and the land.

Water-Based Spirituality

In water-based spiritual practices — from African and Caribbean traditions that honor water deities, to Celtic rituals at holy wells and springs — water represents purification, fertility, and the flow of life. Bathing rituals, moon ceremonies, and offerings to rivers or oceans are central acts of devotion. The Sacral Chakra aligns with these practices as the energetic expression of our bond with the waters that sustain body, soul, and spirit.

A Shared Understanding

Whether through yogic philosophy, shamanic ceremony, indigenous ritual, or earth-based water spirituality, the teaching is clear: we are sustained by flow, and our vitality depends on honoring the waters within and around us. **Svadhisthana** is the chakra that reminds us of this timeless truth: to feel is to live, to create is to honor life, and to flow is to remain connected to the great river of existence.

ORIGINS & HIDDEN HISTORY OF SVADHISTHANA

The concept of **Svadhisthana** arises from the ancient yogic traditions of India, where the chakra system was first described in the **Tantras**. Texts such as the *Sat-Cakra-Nirupana* (circa 16th century) describe Svadhisthana as a **six-petaled lotus**, glowing orange, located in the lower abdomen. Within this lotus, the crescent moon symbolizes cycles, water, and change, while the circle represents the eternal flow of creation and dissolution. Together, they illustrate Svadhisthana as the energetic seat of emotions, creativity, and sensuality.

But the idea of a sacred center for pleasure, fertility, and creative flow is not exclusive to yogic teachings. Traces of sacral wisdom appear across cultures and centuries:

- **Vedic India:** Early hymns honored *rasa* — the "essence" or juice of life — in poetry, ritual, and art. This concept of flow and sweetness directly echoes Svadhisthana's role as the wellspring of vitality and creative joy.
- **Egyptian Mysteries:** Ancient Egypt revered fertility gods and the life-giving Nile. Symbols of Isis and Hathor embody sensuality, motherhood, and the power of emotions — qualities mirrored in the sacral chakra.
- **Greek Philosophy:** Philosophers such as Heraclitus described water as the element of change, reflecting life's constant flow. The myths of Aphrodite also celebrated love, passion, and desire.
- **Chinese Medicine:** In Traditional Chinese Medicine, the *Dan Tian* (lower energy center below the navel) governs vitality, sexuality, and creative force — closely paralleling Svadhisthana's role.
- **Kabbalistic Mysticism:** The sefirah *Yesod*, meaning "Foundation," represents sexuality, imagination, and the unconscious — a symbolic counterpart to the sacral chakra.

Over time, Svadhisthana became associated not only with desire and fertility but also with **spiritual transformation**. Yogic adepts taught that this chakra houses the waters of creation — emotions that, when balanced, fuel Kundalini's rise. To awaken higher consciousness, one must not reject pleasure or feeling, but rather honor them as sacred currents of life.

The "hidden history" of Svadhisthana lies in how societies have treated emotion, sexuality, and creative expression. In cultures where pleasure and intimacy were honored, rituals of fertility, art, and dance flourished. In cultures that repressed or shamed these aspects of life, collective wounds formed — carried forward as guilt, fear of desire, or creative stagnation. These wounds still echo today in sexual taboos, body shame, and emotional suppression.

Understanding Svadhisthana's origins is more than learning its symbols. It is about remembering that creativity, intimacy, and feeling have always been sacred. Pleasure is not a distraction from spiritual life — it is part of the sacred flow from which higher awareness and deeper connection arise.

The Symbolism of the Sacral Chakra

Svadhisthana is associated with the element of **water**, the most fluid and adaptable of all the elements. Water represents movement, change, and emotional depth — the qualities that allow us to feel, connect, and create. Just as the body cannot live without fluids, the spirit cannot awaken without the flowing vitality of Svadhisthana.

Its color is **vibrant orange**, the hue of creativity and life's sweetness. Orange blends the energy of red with the joy of yellow, symbolizing passion transformed into pleasure, survival refined into expression. It is the color of ripe fruit, sunsets, and the inner fire that warms rather than burns. This orange vibration connects us to desire, stirs our imagination, and reminds us that life is meant to be felt and enjoyed.

THE ORANGE LOTUS

The lotus of Svadhisthana is always depicted as **orange**, glowing with vitality and creative fire. Its **six petals** symbolize the six states of mind and emotion that must be balanced: anger, jealousy, cruelty, hatred, pride, and desire. Within the lotus rests a **crescent moon cradling a circle**, representing the cyclical rhythms of the moon, tides, fertility, and creation.

Unlike the red lotus of Muladhara, which anchors us to the ground, the orange lotus of Svadhisthana teaches us to flow, to adapt, and to embrace the cycles of life. It is not the flower of stillness but of movement; not of endurance, but of expression.

Where the root reminds us we are alive, the sacral reminds us life is to be *lived fully*.

THE COLOR ORANGE OF SVADHISTHANA

When you close your eyes and visualize the Sacral Chakra, the color most often seen is **vibrant orange**. This is not merely symbolic but reflects a vibrational truth recognized across Tantric, yogic, and healing traditions. Orange carries the resonance of water energy, creativity, and emotional flow — the very essence of Svadhisthana.

ORANGE: FLOW, CREATIVITY, AND PLEASURE

- **The Color of Vitality and Joy:** Orange blends the primal energy of red with the uplifting brightness of yellow. It is the color of sunsets, ripe fruit, and inner warmth — symbols of life's sweetness and the joy of embodiment.
- **The Waters of Emotion:** Orange mirrors the movement of water, the element of Svadhisthana. Just as rivers flow and adapt, emotions must move through us freely to keep energy balanced.
- **Passion and Desire:** Orange stirs the senses and awakens intimacy. It invites us to experience the body not only as a vessel for survival, but as a sacred temple for pleasure and creative expression.
- **Inspiration and Expression:** Orange stimulates imagination, encouraging art, music, dance, and all forms of creative release. It embodies the spark of passion transformed into expression.

WHY ORANGE BELONGS TO THE SACRAL

Each chakra color resonates with a frequency of light, forming part of the rainbow spectrum that mirrors the human energy system. Orange vibrates just above red, representing energy in motion — life rising beyond survival into flow and feeling.

- **The Second Color of the Rainbow:** Just as orange follows red, Svadhisthana follows Muladhara in the chakra system — the natural next step after safety is established.
- **A Balanced Frequency:** Orange carries more energy than red, yet is gentler than yellow. It is the perfect midpoint between grounding and empowerment, reflecting emotional and creative balance.

- **Fluid and Expansive:** Orange energy moves outward and upward, reminding us that once rooted in safety, we are free to flow into connection, intimacy, and joy.

ORANGE IN DAILY LIFE

- **When you feel emotionally stuck:** Wear orange clothing or jewelry to encourage flow, joy, and creative expression.
- **When your creativity feels blocked:** Visualize breathing in orange light, filling your abdomen with inspiration and passion.
- **When intimacy feels difficult:** Place your hands gently on your lower belly and imagine orange energy radiating warmth, trust, and openness.
- **In rituals of flow and pleasure:** Use orange candles, orange stones (like carnelian or orange calcite), or orange fabrics to amplify the fluid, sensual qualities of Svadhisthana.

MEDITATION WITH ORANGE

1. Close your eyes and visualize a glowing orange lotus just below your navel.
2. See the orange light spreading through your hips, pelvis, and lower abdomen like warm, flowing water.
3. With every breath, imagine this orange energy softening your emotions and awakening your creativity, reminding you:
   "I am free to feel. I am creative. I flow with life."

WANT TO EXPERIENCE IT IN ACTION?...
Watch this video for the Sacral Chakra Meditation.

Watch it here: https://youtu.be/sp8vnb8_g8g

THE DEEPER LESSON OF ORANGE

Orange teaches us that pleasure, creativity, and emotion are not separate from the sacred. To feel deeply, to create boldly, to embrace intimacy, and to delight in life's sweetness — these too are spiritual acts when honored as divine. Just as water must flow for life to flourish, the soul must move with the currents of feeling and creativity to awaken fully.

The Sacral's orange light is both a gift and a reminder. It is the warm glow that says, *"You are allowed to feel. You are allowed to create. You are free to flow with life."*

The Six-Petaled Lotus of Svadhisthana

At the heart of Svadhisthana's symbolism lies an **orange lotus with six petals**, more intricate than the Root but still simple compared to higher chakras. Each petal represents a subtle quality of the human emotional experience. Together, these six petals remind us that creativity and intimacy arise only when emotional flow is balanced.

The Six Syllables

Each petal of Svadhisthana is inscribed with a Sanskrit seed sound: **baṁ, bhaṁ, maṁ, yaṁ, raṁ, and laṁ.** These bija syllables are not mere letters but vibrational codes. Chanting or visualizing them harmonizes the sacral chakra with the flow of life force, cleansing stagnant emotions and opening channels of creativity.

The Six Qualities of Emotion

The six petals are also associated with six tendencies that must be purified or transformed:

- **Anger** – when repressed, it hardens; when expressed with awareness, it fuels creativity.
- **Jealousy** – born of comparison, yet teaching us to honor our unique gifts.
- **Cruelty** – the distortion of desire; balanced, it becomes passion expressed with care.
- **Hatred** – the shadow of intimacy; healed, it becomes discernment and healthy boundaries.
- **Pride** – attachment to the self-image; when balanced, it supports self-worth without arrogance.
- **Desire** – the longing that binds; when purified, it becomes the sacred urge to create and connect.

Together, these petals form the **emotional foundation of human connection**. When any one quality dominates unchecked, relationships and creativity falter. When balanced, emotions become teachers that guide us into intimacy, joy, and artistic flow.

The Six Directions of Flow

The six petals can also be seen as **directions of emotional movement** — forward and back, left and right, inward and outward. This reflects the nature of Svadhisthana as the chakra of exchange: giving and receiving love, feeling and expressing, ebbing and flowing. It teaches us that emotions are not static but currents, and balance comes from movement, not suppression.

The Six Cycles

In another interpretation, the six petals symbolize **cycles of life** — birth, growth, maturity, decline, death, and renewal. Just as water constantly shifts between states (ice, liquid, vapor), our emotions and desires transform across time. Svadhisthana teaches us to embrace these cycles without clinging or resisting, knowing that every ending carries the seed of a new beginning.

The Sacred Geometry of Six

The number six itself holds deep meaning. In sacred geometry, six represents harmony, beauty, and balance — seen in the hexagon of a honeycomb or the six-pointed star. In the sacral chakra, this harmony expresses through relationships, intimacy, and the creative union of opposites. It is the reminder that wholeness is found not in isolation but in connection and flow.

Balance and Flow

Across these interpretations, the six-petaled lotus conveys one central truth: without emotional balance, creativity and intimacy cannot thrive. Just as the Root's four petals embody stability, Svadhisthana's six petals embody fluidity and harmony. This lotus teaches us that true pleasure is not indulgence, but balance — the sacred rhythm of giving and receiving, of ebb and flow.

THE CIRCLE AND THE CRESCENT: SVADHISTHANA'S CORE GEOMETRY

At the very heart of Svadhisthana's lotus lies a **circle cradled by a crescent moon**. Unlike the Root Chakra's square and triangle, which emphasize stability and grounding, the geometry of the Sacral Chakra highlights flow, cycles, and the fluid nature of being. These forms hold profound meaning, symbolizing the essential truths of emotion, creativity, and the waters of life.

The Circle

- The circle is the **universal symbol of wholeness and eternity**. Without beginning or end, it reflects the cycles of life — birth, death, and rebirth — as well as the continuity of emotions and creativity.

- In Tantric cosmology, the circle represents **water**, the element of Svadhisthana, constantly moving and adapting.
- The circle is also linked to **sexuality and creation**, symbolizing the womb as the vessel of life, where new possibilities are conceived and nurtured.
- Unlike the rigid stability of the square in Muladhara, the circle shows us that **life is not fixed** — it moves in cycles, waves, and spirals, teaching us to adapt and flow.

The Crescent Moon

- Resting within the circle is the **crescent moon**, the ancient symbol of fertility, intuition, and the lunar cycles that govern tides, menstruation, and emotional rhythms.
- The crescent emphasizes the **waxing and waning of energy**, reminding us that creativity and desire rise and fall in natural phases.
- In Tantric symbolism, the crescent also represents **flowing consciousness** — the awareness that feelings and sensations are temporary, yet sacred.
- Just as the moon reflects the sun's light, our emotions reflect deeper truths of the soul.

Union of Circle and Crescent

Together, the circle and crescent express a fundamental spiritual truth:

- The **circle** reminds us of continuity, cycles, and wholeness.
- The **crescent** reminds us of phases, fluidity, and change.

When combined, they show that **true vitality comes from honoring both constancy and change**. Life is not about clinging to permanence or fearing shifts, but about learning to ride the tides of experience with grace.

Returning to Flow

While the Root Chakra's geometry points downward into grounding and stability, the Sacral Chakra's geometry invites us into **movement, adaptation, and creative flow**. It teaches that just as water sustains life by flowing, our emotions and creativity sustain the soul by moving freely. Spirit and feeling are not separate — they are two halves of the same truth, meeting in Svadhisthana.

This is the secret wisdom of the Sacral: to be human is to **flow as well as to endure, to feel as well as to survive, to create as well as to exist**.

CIRCLES IN TAROT SYMBOLISM
The Major Arcana

- **The Wheel of Fortune (X):** A literal circle, representing cycles of change, fate, and the eternal turning of life's wheel. This directly mirrors the sacral chakra's lesson: flow is constant, and all things rise and fall.
- **The World (XXI):** Encased in a wreath forming an oval (a circle's counterpart), symbolizing completion, wholeness, and the union of opposites — echoing sacral balance in relationships and creation.
- **The Moon (XVIII):** The crescent moon, central to Svadhisthana's geometry, appears here as a symbol of cycles, illusion, intuition, and emotional tides.

The Minor Arcana

- **The Suit of Cups:** Cups are vessels, but often illustrated as circular bowls or chalices. They represent emotions, relationships, and intuition — all sacral themes. Circles of water (ripples, waves) frequently appear around Cups cards, echoing emotional flow.

- **The Suit of Pentacles:** Pentacles themselves are drawn as five-pointed stars inside a circle, symbolizing material wholeness and manifestation. While more aligned with grounding (Root/earth), they also share the sacral's creative aspect — making ideas tangible.

Sacral Reflections in Circular Imagery

- **Cycles:** Circles in Tarot emphasize life's repeating rhythms — fortune, growth, endings, beginnings. These reflect the sacral chakra's watery lesson: emotions and creativity ebb and flow.
- **Wholeness:** Circles suggest unity and completion, teaching that relationships and creativity are paths to experiencing the fullness of life.
- **Flow:** Whenever water is depicted as rippling outward in circles (e.g., in the Ace of Cups), it mirrors the way emotional energy radiates from Svadhisthana.

KEY CARDS TO MEDITATE ON FOR THE SACRAL CHAKRA

- **The Wheel of Fortune (X):** Embracing cycles of change.
- **The Moon (XVIII):** Honoring emotions, intuition, and the subconscious.
- **The World (XXI):** Feeling complete, integrated, whole.
- **Ace of Cups:** Emotional renewal and opening to flow.
- **Two of Cups:** Sacred union, intimacy, and trust.

Svadhisthana is both the flow and the fuel of the journey. It is the second chakra to awaken in early childhood, carrying the memory of pleasure, intimacy, and emotional response into all later experiences. It is also the ever-present current that nourishes our creativity, relationships, and capacity to feel alive no matter how far we advance on the spiritual path. Without Svadhisthana, the chakra system becomes dry and rigid, like a riverbed without water. With it, we gain the freedom to feel, to create, and to connect — allowing life to move through us with vitality and grace.

In this way, Svadhisthana is not simply a stage to pass through — it is a lifelong teacher. Every act of creation, every moment of intimacy, every wave of emotion is touched by its energy. As we rise toward empowerment, love, and vision, the sacral chakra reminds us that enlightenment is not denial of desire but the **sanctification of feeling and flow.**

Svadhisthana in Yogic Practice

In the earliest **Tantric and yogic traditions**, the chakras were not seen as physical organs but as **subtle energy centers** — focal points for meditation, mantra, and spiritual awakening. Yogis engaged each chakra through visualization, breath, and awareness, awakening deeper layers of consciousness.

For **Svadhisthana, the Sacral Chakra**, practice is centered on **fluidity, creativity, and emotional balance**. The **bija mantra**, or "seed sound," of Svadhisthana is **VAM** — a vibrational key said to activate the water element and harmonize emotional flow. Meditating on the six-petaled lotus and chanting "VAM" connected practitioners to the sacred qualities of pleasure, intimacy, and creative life-force.

The goal was not indulgence, but **purification and alignment**. Yogis understood that emotions, desires, and creativity could either bind the soul or liberate it, depending on whether they were unconscious or consciously integrated. By working with Svadhisthana, practitioners learned to honor desire as sacred energy, transforming it into vitality that supports the rise of kundalini and the awakening of higher consciousness.

THE INNER SYMBOL OF SVADHISTHANA

At the center of Svadhisthana's lotus rests a **crescent moon within a circle**, surrounded by six petals inscribed with Sanskrit syllables. The **crescent moon** represents the cycles of time, tides, and fertility; the **circle** represents continuity, flow, and the eternal rhythms of life. Within this imagery lies the bija mantra **VAM (वं)**, the vibrational essence of creative flow and emotional freedom.

WHAT VAM REPRESENTS

- **Vibrational Key:** VAM is the sound that "unlocks" the Sacral Chakra, awakening creativity, intimacy, and emotional release.
- **Sound of Flow:** When chanted, VAM resonates through the lower abdomen and pelvis, stirring the waters of life and rebalancing emotions.
- **Dissolver of Guilt and Shame:** Ancient teachings describe VAM as a purifier of emotional repression, freeing us from guilt, shame, or fear surrounding intimacy and pleasure.
- **Link to the Water Element:** Each chakra aligns with an element; Svadhisthana is tied to water (*apas tattva*). VAM harmonizes us with adaptability, cleansing, and the ever-changing tides of feeling.

Through the practice of meditating on Svadhisthana's lotus and chanting **VAM**, yogis learned to embrace the full spectrum of human feeling — from joy to grief, desire to creativity — and to flow with these energies rather than resist them. The Sacral Chakra was not viewed as lower or impure, but as the **river of life-force** that nourishes both body and soul. Without its flowing waters, spiritual growth withers; with them, consciousness awakens in beauty, intimacy, and creative abundance.

THE SEED SOUND OF SVADHISTHANA: VAM

At the very center of the Sacral Chakra's symbol lies not only imagery and geometry, but also **sound**. In Tantric teachings, every chakra has a **bija mantra** — a "seed sound" said to contain the vibrational essence of that energy center. For **Svadhisthana, the Sacral Chakra**, the bija is **VAM** (pronounced "Vahm," with an open "ah" sound).

Why Sound Matters

In the Sanskrit tradition, **sound is creation**. It is vibration, frequency, and energy condensed into an audible form. The universe itself, according to yogic philosophy, began with the primal sound **OM**. In the same way, each chakra has a specific vibrational "key" that activates its energy.

For Svadhisthana, that sound is **VAM**. Chanting it is like striking the exact note that awakens emotional flow, dissolves repression, and restores the natural rhythm of creativity and intimacy.

The Power Of Vam

- **Resonance in the Lower Abdomen:** When chanted, VAM vibrates through the pelvis and lower belly, stimulating the waters of the sacral chakra and rebalancing emotional energy.
- **Releasing Guilt and Shame:** Emotional repression, guilt, or shame can block Svadhisthana. VAM clears these stagnant vibrations, creating openness and freedom to feel.
- **Awakening Creativity:** VAM stirs the imagination, helping inspiration rise from the subconscious into conscious expression.

- **Honoring Flow:** The sound aligns us with the element of water, reminding us to move with cycles, tides, and feelings instead of resisting them.

Chanting **VAM** is a practice of permission — the permission to feel, to desire, to create, and to flow. It is the vibrational key that unlocks the sacred dwelling place within, opening the door to pleasure, creativity, and emotional freedom.

HOW TO CHANT VAM

Step 1 – Prepare the Body

- Sit cross-legged or with feet flat on the floor.
- Place your hands gently on your lower abdomen, just below the navel.
- Take 3–5 slow breaths, feeling your belly rise and fall like gentle waves.

Step 2 – Focus on the Sacral

- Visualize a glowing **orange lotus** in the lower abdomen.
- See it shimmering like warm sunlight reflected on water, moving with each breath.
- Imagine the energy flowing like a river through your hips, pelvis, and lower belly.

Step 3 – Chant the Sound

- Inhale deeply. As you exhale, chant: **VAAAAHHHHMmmmm…**
- Allow the "Vah" to flow smoothly on the exhale, then let the "mmm" vibrate gently in the lower abdomen.
- Feel the sound ripple like water, softening emotions and awakening creativity.

Step 4 – Repeat Rhythmically

- Chant **VAM** 7, 12, or 108 times.
- With each repetition, imagine the six lotus petals opening, releasing emotional blockages and radiating joy, intimacy, and creative power.

Step 5 – Silent Resonance

- After chanting, sit quietly.
- Place your awareness in the lower abdomen.
- Feel the subtle vibration of **VAM** flowing like a current of orange light through your whole being — reminding you:
  "I am free to feel. I am creative. I flow with life."

WAYS TO USE VAM IN PRACTICE

- **Morning Flow:** Chant **VAM** three times upon waking to invite creativity, joy, and emotional balance into your day.
- **Emotional Release:** When feeling blocked, numb, or overwhelmed, chant **VAM** until your breath feels fluid and your emotions begin to soften.
- **Healing Sessions:** Practitioners may chant **VAM** silently while working near the hips, lower belly, or sacrum to encourage flow and release.
- **Movement Integration:** Combine chanting with hip-opening yoga poses (like Goddess, Pigeon, or Bound Angle), or with swaying, dancing, or pelvic tilts to embody fluidity.
- **Group Practice:** Chanting **VAM** together magnifies the flow of emotional energy, creating a collective field of creativity, intimacy, and trust.

SACRAL-CENTERED AFFIRMATION WITH VAM

"As I chant VAM, I flow freely. I am creative. I am open to joy, intimacy, and emotional truth."

The Animal Symbol of Svadhisthana: The Crocodile (Makara)

At the base of each chakra lotus, a symbolic animal is depicted. For the **Sacral Chakra**, the guardian and carrier of its energy is the **crocodile**, also called *Makara* in Sanskrit.

WHY THE CROCODILE?

- **Primal Energy:** The crocodile embodies raw, instinctual power — ancient, untamed, and deeply connected to survival. It represents the primal urges that live in the waters of our subconscious.
- **Water Element:** As a creature of rivers and swamps, the crocodile reflects Svadhisthana's element of **water** — fluid, shifting, life-giving yet dangerous if uncontrolled.
- **Dormant Desires:** Just as a crocodile lies still beneath the water's surface until it suddenly moves with force, our emotions and desires may remain hidden until triggered. The sacral chakra governs this ebb and surge of feeling.
- **Fertility and Creation:** In Hindu and Tantric symbolism, the *Makara* is also a mythic water creature, part crocodile and part fish, representing the fertility of rivers and the endless power of life to renew itself.

THE SHADOW OF THE CROCODILE

The crocodile also represents the challenges of Svadhisthana:

- **Unconscious Drives:** Desires that control us when left unchecked.
- **Emotional Overwhelm:** Like floodwaters, emotions can drown balance when not directed with awareness.
- **Addiction or Excess:** The crocodile's hunger symbolizes cravings that consume rather than nourish.

THE WISDOM OF THE CROCODILE

Balanced, the crocodile teaches us:

- **Power in Stillness:** Like the crocodile conserving energy, we can learn to rest deeply and act with precision when the time is right.
- **Trust in Cycles:** The crocodile has survived for millions of years by adapting. So too, we must trust the cycles of emotion, creativity, and intimacy.
- **Sacred Instinct:** Our desires and emotions are not enemies — they are guides. When honored and integrated, they fuel creation, intimacy, and spiritual growth.

MAKARA IN TANTRIC SYMBOLISM

In Tantric depictions of the six-petaled lotus of Svadhisthana, the crocodile (*Makara*) is drawn beneath the lotus. It is said to be the "vehicle" of **Varuna**, the Vedic god of water, reminding us that our emotions and desires are meant to be navigated like rivers — powerful when respected, destructive when ignored.

MEDITATING ON THE CROCODILE

- **Visualization:** Imagine a crocodile resting in still water, its body almost invisible beneath the surface. This is your sacral energy: deep, powerful, waiting.
- **Affirmation:** *"I honor my instincts. I ride the waters of emotion with awareness and trust."*
- **Integration:** Work with water imagery — flowing rivers, tides, moon cycles — to understand your own emotional depths.

The Deities of the Sacral Chakra

In **Tantric tradition**, each chakra is presided over by deities who embody its essential qualities. These figures are not merely external gods to be worshipped, but **inner archetypes** — reflections of the subtle energies within us that can be awakened through meditation and practice.

For **Svadhisthana, the Sacral Chakra**, the presiding deities embody themes of **water, desire, creativity, fertility, and the flowing cycles of life**.

VISHNU – THE PRESERVER OF FLOW AND HARMONY

- Vishnu, the preserver and sustainer in the Hindu trinity, is often associated with Svadhisthana as its presiding male deity.
- Just as Vishnu maintains cosmic order, in the Sacral Chakra, he symbolizes the **sustaining flow of life-energy** — emotions, desires, and creative impulses that must be honored and balanced.
- He represents continuity, adaptability, and the ability to remain centered even as life moves in cycles of change.

- Meditating on Vishnu within Svadhisthana awakens the wisdom of **trusting the flow** — knowing that emotions, like rivers, cleanse and carry us toward renewal.

RAKINI – THE SHAKTI OF SVADHISTHANA

- The feminine guardian of the Sacral Chakra is **Rakini**, a goddess of sensuality, creativity, and sacred emotion.
- She is often depicted with a radiant orange glow, holding a lotus and a musical instrument — symbols of fertility, rhythm, and artistic expression.
- Rakini embodies the power of desire, not as indulgence but as **life-force energy** that fuels intimacy, passion, and creation.
- As the awakened feminine of Svadhisthana, she teaches us to embrace our feelings, sexuality, and creative cycles as sacred, rather than sources of shame.

TOGETHER: VISHNU AND RAKINI

Together, Vishnu and Rakini balance the Sacral Chakra's dual nature:

- **Vishnu** provides order, harmony, and the sustaining flow that carries emotions and desires into balance.
- **Rakini** provides vitality, passion, and the creative Shakti that animates and expresses those energies.

Their union reminds us that **to flow is not to be chaotic** — it is the sacred dance of form and feeling, order and passion, water and fire. When these archetypes are awakened within us, we reclaim our right to feel, to create, and to experience intimacy as a pathway to the divine.

SACRAL DEITIES IN OTHER TRADITIONS

Though Tantra specifically names **Vishnu** and **Rakini** as the guardians of Svadhisthana, many cultures and traditions personify the qualities of the Sacral Chakra through their own sacred figures:

- **In Hindu culture**, the river goddesses such as **Ganga** and **Yamuna** embody the purifying, flowing, and fertile qualities of water, paralleling Svadhisthana's role as the center of emotional cleansing and renewal.
- **In Indigenous cosmologies**, water spirits and moon deities represent fertility, cycles, and the emotional tides of life. They remind us that creativity and intimacy are born from harmony with the waters of the earth.
- **In Western mysticism**, the Sacral finds resonance with **Archangel Gabriel**, often associated with water, the moon, and creative inspiration. Gabriel is the messenger of divine truth, awakening intuition and emotional clarity.
- **In Egyptian tradition**, the goddess **Hathor** embodies love, pleasure, music, and fertility — all central themes of the sacral energy. She reflects the joy and sensuality of life as sacred expressions of divinity.

These parallels reveal a **universal recognition**: across cultures, the Sacral Chakra is guided by deities and archetypes of **water, fertility, creativity, and emotional flow.**

The Element of Svadhisthana: Water (Apas)

Each chakra is traditionally aligned with one of the five great elements of nature (*pancha mahabhutas*). For the **Sacral Chakra**, that element is **water — Apas** in Sanskrit. This is not mere symbolism but a direct reflection of Svadhisthana's qualities: **flow, adaptability, pleasure, and emotional movement.**

WATER AS THE FLOW OF LIFE

Water is fluid. It moves, adapts, and nourishes. It is the rivers that shape the land, the rain that renews the earth, and the oceans that cradle the mystery of life itself. Just as the Sacral Chakra governs movement and creativity, water represents the vital currents that keep life in motion.

- **Fluidity and Adaptability:** Water flows into every shape and space, teaching us to adapt with grace. When Svadhisthana is balanced, emotions flow freely without being dammed or overwhelming.
- **Pleasure and Nourishment:** Water refreshes, cleanses, and delights. In the Sacral Chakra, it represents our right to feel joy, intimacy, and sensual pleasure as nourishment for the soul.
- **Cycles and Tides:** Water is never static — it evaporates, rains, collects, and flows again. Svadhisthana aligns us with these cycles: the ebb and flow of emotions, creativity, sexuality, and relationships.

Balanced, the water of Svadhisthana cleanses and enlivens us. Blocked, it stagnates into repression, guilt, or rigidity. Overactive, it floods us with overwhelming emotions or addictive patterns. Like water itself, this chakra teaches us the sacred art of **flow — not resisting life's currents, but moving with them.**

WHY WATER BELONGS TO THE SACRAL

The chakras ascend through the elements: **earth (root), water (sacral), fire (solar plexus), air (heart), and ether/space (throat)**, each becoming lighter and more subtle. After the grounding solidity of earth, water is the natural progression — the element of **movement, adaptability, and flow.**

Water belongs to Svadhisthana because this chakra governs the tides of our inner world: **emotions, creativity, sexuality, and relationships.** Just as rivers carve valleys and oceans shape coastlines, our feelings and desires shape the journey of our lives.

Svadhisthana asks us to:

- **Flow rather than resist.**
- **Adapt rather than cling.**
- **Embrace cycles rather than fear change.**

Water is the element of **fluid embodiment** — the commitment to feel, to create, and to move with life's rhythms instead of against them.

MEDITATING ON WATER

Bringing the element of water into Sacral Chakra practices awakens fluidity and release:

1. **Water Visualization:** Sit comfortably and imagine an **orange crescent moon floating in rippling water** in your lower abdomen. With each breath, see the ripples expand, carrying away old emotional heaviness.

2. **Flowing Movement:** Put on soft music and allow your hips and body to sway like waves. Each movement reminds your nervous system: *"I am free to feel. I flow with life."*

3. **Water Connection:** Place your hands in a bowl of water or stand near a river, lake, or ocean. Feel the coolness, the movement, the vitality of water. Whisper: *"I am fluid. I am creative. I am renewed."*

WATER IN DAILY LIFE

- **When emotions feel stuck:** Drink a full glass of water slowly, imagining it washing through your body and clearing away stagnant feelings.
- **When you feel creatively blocked:** Take a shower, bath, or swim. Let the flow of water awaken inspiration and imagination.
- **When intimacy feels difficult:** Sit near a river, lake, or ocean. Breathe with the rhythm of the waves, allowing your body to remember the natural ebb and flow of closeness.
- **When life feels rigid or dry:** Dance, sway, or move your hips in circles. Reclaim your natural fluidity and playfulness.

THE LESSON OF WATER

Water reminds us that true strength is found in flexibility, not in force. Just as rivers carve mountains over time, our emotions and creativity shape the landscape of our lives when allowed to flow freely. Svadhisthana teaches us that intimacy, pleasure, and emotional movement are not indulgences — they are the sacred currents that give life its richness and beauty.

A Sacral Chakra aligned with water becomes an ocean: vast, renewing, and boundless.

BRINGING THE SYMBOLS TOGETHER

Taken together, these symbols form a complete picture of the Sacral Chakra's role:

- The **six lotus petals** reflect the energies of desire, creativity, and emotional balance.
- The **circle and crescent moon** embody cycles, fluidity, and renewal.
- The **crocodile (makara)** symbolizes instinct, depth, and primal life-force.
- The **color orange** glows with vitality, joy, and creative power.

To meditate on these symbols is to invite their qualities into your own life. Each image is a reminder that flow is sacred — a living relationship with your emotions, your creativity, and the waters of life itself.

THE SACRAL AS THE SACRED POOL

Long before chakras were drawn as wheels of light or lotus mandalas, the sages described **Svadhisthana** as a hidden pool deep within the body. It was imagined not as solid earth, but as a shimmering **inner reservoir of water** — a sacred lake of the soul — where the currents of emotion and creativity flow.

The Pool Within

Where the Root was envisioned as an underground cavern, the Sacral was described as a **subterranean spring**, fed by the waters of life itself. Yogis taught that if you follow awareness into the lower belly, beneath the shifting surface of desires and emotions, you arrive at this pool.

Here, at the base of the pelvis, the waters of creativity gather. This pool is not stagnant — it moves, swirls, and reflects. It is the womb of both **pleasure and creation**, a fertile source where life renews itself through intimacy, imagination, and flow.

Why the Sacral?

The Sacral is the seat of fluid embodiment — the place where the self learns to feel, to desire, to express, and to connect. To enter its pool is to touch a primal truth: **you are meant to move, to create, to feel alive.**

- **In Tantra:** Svadhisthana is the dwelling place of the subtle waters (*apas tattva*), the currents of Shakti that cleanse and enliven.
- **In Yoga:** It is the "sweet place," the second support, where pleasure and flow sustain the journey toward higher states.
- **In Indigenous Mysticism:** Sacred lakes, rivers, and wells are seen as portals to the unseen — entrances to fertility, renewal, and the mystery of the ancestors.

A Shared Wisdom

Across cultures, the Sacral has always been linked to **water** — to springs, rivers, wombs, and the shimmering spaces where life begins anew. Where the Root anchors us in the earth, the Sacral invites us into the flow of feeling, reminding us that creation itself begins in the waters of life.

THE SACRAL CHAKRA AS A MAP

The Sacral Chakra's lotus — with its six petals, circle, and crescent moon — can be seen as a symbolic **map into the inner waters**. The petals are the waves of emotion, the circle is the vessel of wholeness, and the crescent is the tide of cycles. Together they guide awareness inward into the **sacred pool of Svadhisthana**, where creativity and intimacy dwell, holding the memory of pleasure and the seed of creation.

A Practice: Entering the Pool

1. Close your eyes. Place your hands gently on your lower abdomen, just below the navel.
2. Imagine a shimmering doorway of light opening into a hidden pool within you.
3. Step inward in your mind's eye, descending into a luminous, orange-lit reservoir.
4. At the center, see the water rippling — alive, fertile, reflecting both your emotions and your creative spark.
5. Sit beside these inner waters with reverence. Know that they are your source of flow, intimacy, and sacred imagination.

The Deeper Lesson

The pool of the Sacral reminds us that spirituality is not about denying feeling, but **embracing flow as divine**. The world may shift, relationships may change, emotions may surge — but beneath it all, there is a reservoir inside you that is endlessly renewing.

To return to this pool is to return to flow.
To live from this pool is to live open, creative, and deeply alive.

THE WESTERN ADAPTATION

When the chakra system was introduced to the West in the late 19th and early 20th centuries, its original Tantric and yogic context was reshaped into concepts Western audiences could more readily embrace. Thinkers such as C.W. Leadbeater and Alice Bailey emphasized the chakras' connections to **psychology, health, and personal development**, rather than focusing solely on their role in subtle body meditation.

In this adaptation, the **Sacral Chakra (Svadhisthana)** came to symbolize **emotions, sexuality, creativity, and relationships**.

Western psychology — particularly the work of Freud and Jung — aligned naturally with these themes. Freud's theories of libido and creative drive, and Jung's exploration of the unconscious and archetypes, both resonate with Svadhisthana's role as the seat of desire, imagination, and emotional flow.

By the mid-20th century, as the New Age movement expanded, healers and energy practitioners began teaching the Sacral Chakra as the center of **pleasure, intimacy, fertility, and artistic expression.** It became associated with issues of guilt, shame, repression, and emotional imbalance. While ancient yogis described Svadhisthana as the dwelling place of water and the cycles of creation, Western teachers often reframed it as a tool for **healing relationships, awakening creativity, and restoring emotional health.**

Today, in Western Reiki, yoga, and holistic practices, the Sacral Chakra is frequently described as the key to **embracing pleasure, releasing guilt, and unlocking creative flow.** Workshops and therapies often focus on connecting with one's sensuality, expressing emotions freely, or rekindling artistic inspiration. Though this sometimes simplifies the deeper esoteric symbolism of Svadhisthana, it remains true to its essence: without flow, intimacy, and emotional connection, human life feels dry and incomplete.

The hidden history of the Sacral shows us that this chakra is not merely about indulgence or romance, but about the **sacred waters of life itself.** As we continue in this book, we will weave together both its ancient yogic origins and modern psychological insights, creating a fuller and more integrated understanding of Svadhisthana's role in awakening vitality, intimacy, and creativity in our lives today.

Archetypes of the Sacral Chakra

Every chakra expresses itself through patterns of thought, feeling, and behavior. These patterns often crystallize into **archetypes** — universal roles or identities that reveal both the light and shadow sides of an energy center. For the **Sacral Chakra**, two archetypes stand out: **The Lover** and **The Creator.**

THE LOVER

The Lover represents Svadhisthana's essence: the longing for intimacy, connection, and pleasure. This archetype embodies sensuality, vulnerability, and the capacity to give and receive emotional depth. The Lover teaches us that joy, desire, and intimacy are not indulgences, but sacred pathways to knowing ourselves and others more deeply.

- **In Balance:** The Lover archetype brings openness, passion, and the ability to form healthy relationships. It embraces vulnerability, allowing for trust, tenderness, and deep emotional connection. People expressing this archetype in balance move through life with a sense of play, attraction, and delight in the beauty of existence.
- **In Shadow:** When distorted, the Lover may manifest as dependency, obsession, or fear of abandonment. It may use intimacy to fill an inner void rather than share a genuine connection. In shadow, the Lover can confuse pleasure with attachment, leading to cycles of guilt, shame, or unhealthy relationships.

The Lover reminds us that true intimacy begins within. To love another deeply, we must first allow ourselves to feel worthy of love.

THE CREATOR

Where the Lover expresses connection, the Creator channels flow into artistry, innovation, and the birthing of new possibilities. This archetype is not limited to artists — it is the energy of creativity in all forms, from ideas and projects to children and communities. The Creator embodies Svadhisthana's role as the womb of imagination and renewal.

- **In Balance:** The Creator is inspired, playful, and expressive. It channels emotions into beauty, movement, and invention, reminding us that creativity is a sacred act of life itself. In balance, the Creator sees obstacles as opportunities for innovation and thrives on curiosity and experimentation.
- **In Shadow:** When unbalanced, the Creator may slip into blockages, self-doubt, or perfectionism. It may repress ideas out of fear of failure, or swing into overindulgence, chasing endless stimulation without true fulfillment. In shadow, the Creator forgets that the flow of inspiration is cyclical and natural.

The Creator reminds us that creativity is not about producing endlessly but about allowing life's currents to move through us freely.

Together, the **Lover** and **Creator** reveal the dual gift of Svadhisthana: the ability to **connect deeply** and to **create abundantly.** One nourishes intimacy, the other expression. Both remind us that flow is sacred, and that embracing pleasure and imagination is a vital part of being human.

LIVING ARCHETYPALLY

Both the **Lover** and the **Creator** live within us. Sometimes one voice rises more strongly than the other, depending on our emotional history, relationships, and creative expression. By recognizing these archetypes, we can see where our energy is flowing freely and where shame, repression, or overindulgence may be distorting the current.

Living archetypally with Svadhisthana means balancing the Lover's openness to intimacy with the Creator's power of expression. Together, they remind us that to feel alive in the world is both to **connect deeply** and to **create freely.**

ROOT ARCHETYPE REFLECTION EXERCISE

The archetypes of the Root Chakra — **The Survivor** and **The Provider** — live in all of us. Sometimes they guide us toward balance and resilience; other times they reveal our fears and imbalances. Reflection helps us recognize where these archetypes show up in our lives and how we can align them with stability and trust.

Take a few quiet moments for this exercise. Find a comfortable position with your feet firmly on the ground. Close your eyes, take three deep breaths, and imagine roots growing downward from your body into the earth. As you feel grounded, reflect on the questions below. Write your responses in a journal, allowing honesty and insight to flow freely.

Exploring the Survivor

1. When have I relied on my inner Survivor to overcome difficulty?
2. How do I respond to uncertainty or crisis — with trust, or with fear?
3. What strengths does my Survivor archetype bring me?

4. In what ways might my Survivor slip into shadow — fear of scarcity, hypervigilance, or constant worry?
5. What grounding practice helps my Survivor feel safe enough to rest?

Exploring the Provider

1. When do I feel most like a Provider — caring for others, offering stability, or creating a safe space?
2. How do I balance my responsibility to others with caring for myself?
3. In what ways do I provide security, resources, or belonging for my family, friends, or community?
4. Where might my Provider archetype become unbalanced — taking on too much, trying to control, or hoarding resources?
5. What would it feel like to trust that I am enough, and that I provide enough?

Integration

- Which archetype feels stronger in me right now — Survivor or Provider?
- Where do I notice shadow patterns in either archetype?
- What small step can I take this week to bring my Root energy into greater balance?

Reflection Mantra:

"I honor the Survivor within me for keeping me alive. I honor the Provider within me for creating safety. Together they root me in trust, stability, and belonging."

Chapter 3 – The Energetic Blueprint of the Sacral

The Sacral Chakra and the Aura

The Sacral Chakra does more than stir our emotions or awaken creativity — it establishes the **energetic currents of flow within the aura**, shaping how we experience intimacy, pleasure, and emotional exchange with the world around us. If the Root gives the aura its foundation, the Sacral gives it **movement, vibrancy, and adaptability.**

When Svadhisthana is strong, the aura glows with a warm orange hue around the lower abdomen and hips, blending fluidly into the surrounding colors of the chakra system. The energy field feels alive, radiant, and magnetic. Others may sense a vitality and openness that draws people in. Emotionally, you feel expressive, adaptable, and able to navigate change without losing balance.

When Svadhisthana is weak or blocked, the aura can appear dull, stagnant, or overly leaky. This may leave you feeling drained after social interactions, creatively uninspired, or emotionally disconnected. People with sacral imbalances often describe cycles of numbness followed by overwhelm, as if their inner waters are either dammed or flooding without control.

The Sacral Chakra **governs the tides of energy within the aura**, just as the moon governs the tides of the ocean. This is why water practices — bathing in natural waters, visualizing orange ripples flowing through the lower belly, or chanting the bija mantra *VAM* — can restore balance. These practices send a signal to Svadhisthana: *I allow myself to feel. I allow myself to flow. I allow myself to create.* In response, the aura regains its fluid rhythm, glowing with vitality and emotional clarity.

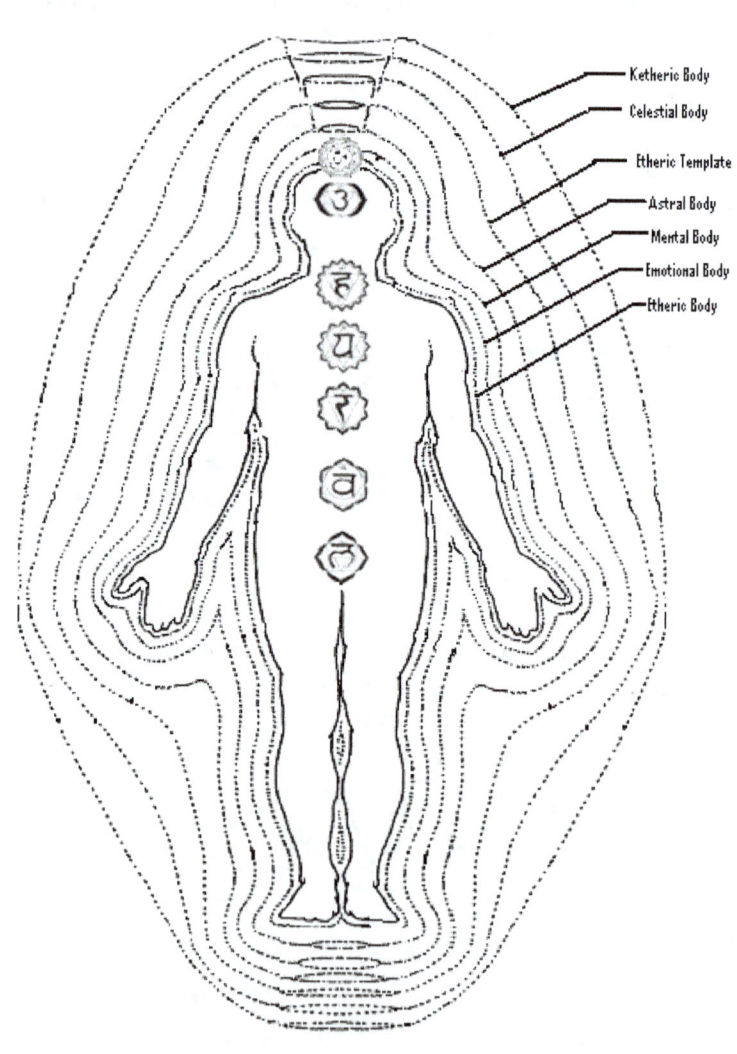

Ketheric Body
Celestial Body
Etheric Template
Astral Body
Mental Body
Emotional Body
Etheric Body

From a practitioner's perspective, the Sacral Chakra is often the first place to explore when someone's aura feels creatively blocked, emotionally stagnant, or prone to unhealthy entanglements. Even if the Root is strong and the upper chakras bright, without flow in Svadhisthana, the aura becomes brittle or disconnected from pleasure. Like a riverbed without water, it cannot nourish life.

In this way, Svadhisthana serves as the **energetic blueprint of flow for the aura** — the inner river that determines whether our energy field can move, cleanse, and renew itself.

Flow of Energy from the Sacral Upward

The Sacral Chakra is not an isolated center of emotions and pleasure — it is the **second gateway** through which life force energy evolves and begins to express itself more fully. In yogic tradition, this current of energy is called **prana**, and in Tantric teachings, it is guided upward by Kundalini as she moves through the body's central channel, the **sushumna nadi**.

At Svadhisthana, the survival energy rooted in Muladhara transforms into something new: **fluidity, intimacy, creativity, and emotional depth.** Once these qualities are awakened, the energy continues its ascent into higher forms of power and expression:

- **From Svadhisthana (Sacral) → to Manipura (Solar Plexus):** Emotional energy and creativity gain focus and become personal power, will, and confidence.
- **From Manipura → to Anahata (Heart):** Power softens into compassion, trust, and unconditional love.
- **From Heart → to Vishuddha (Throat):** Love finds its voice, becoming authentic expression and truth.
- **From Throat → upward:** Expression leads to insight, vision, and ultimately transcendence.

This rising current reflects a universal truth: **life unfolds in cycles of increasing refinement.** Desire precedes empowerment, empowerment precedes love, and love precedes vision. Just as water must flow before it can nourish crops, our emotions and creativity must flow before higher consciousness can blossom.

When Svadhisthana is balanced, this upward flow is smooth, nourishing each chakra with the energy of creativity and emotional vitality. But when the Sacral is blocked, repressed, or unstable, the entire system above it suffers. Power at the solar plexus may feel forced, love at the heart may feel closed, and expression at the throat may become rigid or distorted.

Practitioners often describe the Sacral as the **inner river** of the chakra system. If the river is dry, the higher centers thirst; if it floods uncontrollably, the upper chakras are overwhelmed. But when it flows in balance, it feeds every part of the energetic body, allowing power, love, and vision to flourish.

The Sacral Chakra does not hold energy captive in the waters of desire — it teaches energy how to **move, adapt, and renew.** Like rivers flowing into the sea, Svadhisthana ensures that the life-force currents rise upward with nourishment, grace, and creativity, carrying the soul toward its highest flowering.

The Sacral as the Seat of Emotion and Desire

If the heart is the seat of love, and the root is the seat of instinct, then the sacral chakra is the **seat of emotion and desire.** Svadhisthana governs the primal currents of pleasure, passion, and creativity — the energies that move us toward connection, reproduction, and the enjoyment of life itself. This is not intellectual reasoning; it is the body's natural rhythm, the ebb and flow of emotion and sensation that remind us we are alive.

From an evolutionary perspective, Svadhisthana reflects the stage of development when survival needs are secured and the human spirit turns toward relationship, intimacy, and creation. Our ancestors, once fed and sheltered, began to form bonds, families, and communities. They danced, sang, made art, and celebrated cycles of fertility and harvest — all expressions of sacral energy. This center is the bridge between survival and flourishing, between merely existing and experiencing life as rich, sensual, and meaningful.

When the Sacral Chakra is in balance, emotions flow freely without overwhelming us. We can feel joy, sadness, desire, or fear without being consumed by them. Desire becomes a guiding force rather than a trap, and creativity feels like a natural extension of living. Relationships are nourished by openness, intimacy, and trust. In this state, Svadhisthana gives us permission to embrace pleasure as sacred — whether through art, sexuality, or the simple joy of being.

When the sacral is out of balance, emotions become distorted. Energy may stagnate, creating numbness, repression, or disconnection from pleasure and creativity. Or it may overflow, leading to emotional volatility, overindulgence, or dependency. Desire, when misaligned, may chase temporary satisfaction instead of deeper fulfillment. In both cases, the life force is present but misdirected, either locked away or spilling out uncontrollably.

Svadhisthana also influences the body's cycles — reproduction, sexuality, and the hormonal tides that shape emotional rhythm. Just as water ebbs and flows, the sacral thrives when emotions are allowed to move in cycles, not frozen or forced. In modern life, however, cultural shame, trauma, and emotional suppression often block this natural flow. Instead of a source of vitality, the sacral becomes a reservoir of unresolved feelings, unexpressed creativity, or unacknowledged desire.

Healing the Sacral Chakra restores emotions to their rightful place: as **currents of connection and creation.** When balanced, Svadhisthana allows us to feel deeply without losing center, to desire without grasping, and to create without fear. We move beyond repression or indulgence into flow — a dance of feeling, expression, and renewal. Not abandoning our emotions, but honoring them as the sacred waters that nourish both body and soul.

A UNIVERSAL UNDERSTANDING OF FLOW

Though the chakra system originates in the yogic traditions of India, the experience of flow is universal. Across cultures and times, human beings have understood the need to connect with water, emotion, and rhythm as the basis of pleasure, creativity, and relationships.

To be in flow is to feel alive, expressive, and connected — to yourself, to your senses, and to the people around you. It is that deep sense of **"I feel. I create. I connect."** Whether through ritual, art, dance, or intimacy, practices of flow arise naturally in every culture because the human spirit instinctively seeks movement after stability, pleasure after survival, and connection after isolation.

- **Indigenous Traditions**: Water rituals, river ceremonies, and moon cycles honor the fluid power of life. Many cultures view water as the womb of creation, reminding us that emotions and fertility are sacred.
- **Shamanic Practices**: Ceremonies often invoke water as a cleansing, healing force. Shamans journey through rivers, lakes, and rain as symbols of emotional release and renewal.

- **Eastern Systems**: In yoga, Svadhisthana is tied to the water element and the flow of prana through the pelvis. Taoist practices emphasize balance of yin and yang — the dance of polarity and union — which mirrors the sacral's themes of intimacy and harmony.
- **Western Mysticism**: The element of Water is linked to emotions, intuition, and creativity. In the Tarot, the suit of Cups reflects the sacral realm — love, pleasure, imagination, and emotional depth.

Even in modern psychology, flow is recognized as vital for wellbeing. Therapists encourage creative expression, emotional regulation, and healthy intimacy as pathways to joy and fulfillment. The concept of *"being in the flow"* is widely understood as a peak state of presence, where creativity and emotion move effortlessly.

What all these perspectives share is the recognition that flow is not merely about pleasure or indulgence. It is both energetic and spiritual. We may suppress emotions, deny pleasure, or block creativity — but if the inner rivers stop flowing, life feels stagnant. True sacral alignment arises when body, mind, and spirit all affirm:
I feel. I flow. I create. I connect.

In this way, flow is both universal and deeply personal. It can be as simple as dancing to a rhythm, painting with color, or sitting by water — yet as profound as awakening the truth that your emotions, your creativity, and your relationships are sacred currents of life itself.

Svadhisthana holds this truth: flow is not a distraction, nor a luxury — it is a gift. The gift of being alive, sensual, and in harmony with the waters of creation.

How Practitioners Work with the Sacral Chakra

For healers and energy practitioners, the Sacral Chakra — *Svadhisthana* — is often seen as the center of flow. Located in the lower abdomen, just below the navel, it governs emotional wellbeing, sensuality, creativity, and the ability to connect with others. When Svadhisthana is in balance, life feels fluid, joyful, and creative. When blocked, emotions stagnate, intimacy becomes difficult, and inspiration dries up.

Assessment

Practitioners begin by tuning into a client's emotional and creative energy. They may ask questions about:

- How emotions are expressed or suppressed.
- Comfort with intimacy, pleasure, and touch.
- Relationship patterns, trust, and vulnerability.
- Creative flow — whether ideas come easily or feel blocked.

Energetically, healers often sense Svadhisthana in the hips, pelvis, and lower belly. A balanced sacral field feels warm, flowing, and radiant, while imbalance may appear as rigidity, heaviness, or chaotic emotional waves.

Energy Healing Techniques

- **Reiki & Hands-On Healing**: Energy is channeled into the lower abdomen, hips, and lower back to restore fluidity and balance.
- **Sound Healing**: The bija mantra *VAM* resonates with Svadhisthana, bringing harmony to emotions and creativity. Flowing instruments like crystal singing bowls, flutes, or water drums are often used.

- **Crystal Healing**: Carnelian, orange calcite, moonstone, amber, and peach selenite are placed over the sacral region to spark creativity and sensuality.
- **Aromatherapy**: Sweet, exotic oils like ylang-ylang, sandalwood, orange, clary sage, and jasmine help open the sacral to pleasure and flow.

Bodywork Practices

Because Svadhisthana is deeply connected to the hips and pelvis, physical movement plays a powerful role in healing:

- **Hip-opening yoga poses** (Goddess Pose, Pigeon Pose, Bound Angle) release stored emotions.
- **Fluid movement practices** like dance, belly dance, or tai chi encourage flow.
- **Massage or reflexology** in the hips, lower belly, or sacral reflex zones releases emotional tension stored in the body.

Spiritual and Ancestral Healing

Practitioners often address emotional and sexual wounds in this chakra:

- **Guided meditations** to release shame, guilt, or fear around pleasure and intimacy.
- **Ancestral healing** to clear inherited patterns of repression, trauma, or broken trust.
- **Water rituals** such as sacred bathing, moon ceremonies, or connecting with rivers and oceans to restore the sacral's elemental balance.

Integration

Healing Svadhisthana is about cultivating practices of flow and allowing pleasure without guilt. Practitioners encourage clients to:

- Create time for play, art, or music.
- Connect with water — through bathing, swimming, or simply drinking with mindfulness.
- Practice mindful intimacy — exploring touch, movement, or connection with presence rather than performance.
- Journal emotions to allow them to flow safely, rather than remain suppressed.

For healers, the Sacral Chakra is where survival becomes experience, where stability transforms into creativity, and where connection deepens into intimacy. It reminds us that **life is not meant only to be endured — it is meant to be felt, expressed, and enjoyed.**

Chapter 4 – Signs of Imbalance

Shadow Aspects of the Sacral Chakra

Every chakra contains both light and shadow. The Sacral Chakra, Svadhisthana, governs creativity, emotion, sensuality, and connection — the fluid essence of being human. Yet when this energy becomes distorted, its flow turns turbulent. Instead of bringing pleasure and creativity, it manifests as emotional instability, repression, or overindulgence.

The shadows of the Sacral Chakra are not to be feared; they are messages from the inner waters, signaling where emotions have been suppressed, boundaries crossed, or joy forgotten. They reveal where life's natural flow has been blocked or flooded.

Emotional Instability

When Svadhisthana is imbalanced, emotions rise and fall like unpredictable tides. Mood swings, emotional numbness, or hypersensitivity may appear. You might feel consumed by feelings one day and detached the next. The waters of emotion have lost rhythm, making it hard to trust your own inner flow.

Creative Block or Overdrive

Creativity is the Sacral's natural expression. When the chakra is underactive, inspiration dries up — ideas feel forced, passion fades, and life loses its color. When overactive, creativity can become scattered or obsessive, burning through energy without

rest or fulfillment. In both cases, the flow is imbalanced —
either dammed or overflowing.

Guilt and Shame

The most common shadow of the Sacral Chakra is guilt —
especially around pleasure, desire, or emotional needs. When
conditioned beliefs teach that joy or sensuality are "wrong," this
chakra contracts. Shame then replaces spontaneity, creating a
split between the body and the soul. Healing begins by
remembering that pleasure and feeling are sacred, not sinful.

Co-dependence and Isolation

The Sacral Chakra governs relationships and intimacy. When its
energy is imbalanced, one may cling too tightly to others,
seeking validation through connection (overactive), or withdraw
entirely, fearing rejection or vulnerability (underactive). Both
extremes stem from the same wound: forgetting one's inner
worth and emotional autonomy.

Addiction and Overindulgence

Because Svadhisthana is the center of pleasure, imbalance can
lead to chasing sensation as a substitute for fulfillment.
Overeating, sexual compulsion, or emotional dependency can
all emerge when the deeper need for authentic joy goes unmet.
These behaviors are not moral failings — they are attempts to
soothe emptiness where flow has been lost.

Creative and Emotional Repression

In some, the Sacral's shadow takes the opposite form —
emotional suppression and denial of pleasure. This often arises
from early conditioning that taught restraint, punishment, or
emotional invalidation. The result is a disconnection from

passion, sensuality, and spontaneity — a life lived in grayscale instead of color.

The Lesson of the Shadows

The shadows of Svadhisthana remind us that emotion and pleasure are not enemies of the spiritual path — they are gateways to wholeness. Healing the Sacral Chakra means learning to flow again: to feel deeply without being swept away, to create freely without fear, and to embrace pleasure as a natural expression of the soul's vitality.

Blocked or Deficient Sacral Energy

When the Sacral Chakra is blocked or deficient, life loses its color and movement. The emotional and creative waters of Svadhisthana become stagnant — either dried up from repression or frozen by fear. Instead of flowing with inspiration and feeling, you may sense emotional emptiness, creative paralysis, or disconnection from pleasure and intimacy.

An underactive Sacral Chakra often develops when emotions, desires, or sensuality have been shamed or suppressed. It is the result of messages like *"Don't cry," "Don't feel,"* or *"Be good, not passionate."* Over time, this conditioning creates a subtle withdrawal from life itself.

Emotional Numbness

When the Sacral is deficient, emotions flatten. Joy feels muted, grief feels unreachable, and passion fades into indifference. You may feel functional but uninspired, moving through routines without true engagement. This emotional shutdown often develops as protection — a defense against old pain or rejection.

Loss of Creativity

Creativity thrives on flow, but when Svadhisthana contracts, inspiration dries up. Ideas that once felt alive may seem out of reach. Artists experience "creative block," while others may feel uninspired in daily life — unable to imagine new possibilities or take pleasure in beauty.

Suppressed Desire and Pleasure

A blocked Sacral Chakra often resists pleasure. Sensuality, intimacy, or even simple enjoyment may trigger guilt or discomfort. Physical connection can feel unsafe, while emotional closeness feels overwhelming. Pleasure itself becomes associated with danger, control, or loss — so the instinct is to shut it down entirely.

Fear of Change and Flow

Because Svadhisthana governs flexibility, an underactive chakra may show up as rigidity — resistance to change, spontaneity, or emotional vulnerability. You may cling to routine or numbness as a way to avoid uncertainty. But in doing so, life's natural currents of creativity and emotion are blocked.

Isolation and Disconnection

When emotional energy is frozen, connection to others weakens. Relationships may feel mechanical or distant, as though something essential is missing. You may long for intimacy but fear being seen or hurt, creating a cycle of longing and withdrawal.

Physical Manifestations

Deficient Sacral energy often manifests in the lower body — hips, pelvis, and reproductive organs. Symptoms may include stiffness, low libido, menstrual irregularities, bladder issues, or chronic fatigue. The body mirrors the energy: tight, depleted, or cold.

The Hidden Wound

At its core, blocked Sacral energy reveals an unhealed wound of rejection — the belief that one's emotions or desires are not welcome. This wound can trace back to childhood environments where feelings were minimized or expression was unsafe. The result is a guarded heart and a closed channel of creativity.

Healing begins not with forcing passion to return, but with gentle permission to feel again.
Small moments of joy — dancing, laughter, touch, or art — reopen the flow.
Like a frozen river in spring, warmth returns slowly but inevitably.

Excess or Overactive Sacral Energy

When the Sacral Chakra becomes overstimulated, its natural fluidity turns into turbulence. Instead of flowing in harmony, emotions, desires, and passions surge uncontrollably — like waves crashing without rhythm or direction. This overactivity can feel intoxicating at first, but it often leads to imbalance, burnout, or emotional instability.

An overactive Svadhisthana usually develops when emotional or sensual energy has been awakened without grounding in the Root Chakra. It can also arise from environments where feelings, indulgence, or drama were overemphasized, teaching the nervous system that intensity equals aliveness. The result is excess movement without containment — flow without form.

Emotional Volatility

When Sacral energy floods the system, emotions swing from ecstasy to despair. You may feel overly reactive, easily triggered, or caught in dramatic highs and lows. Relationships can become chaotic, fueled by passion one moment and conflict the next. Instead of emotional expression bringing release, it becomes consuming.

Overindulgence and Addiction

An unbalanced Sacral Chakra may crave constant stimulation — through food, sex, spending, or thrill-seeking. Pleasure becomes a way to escape emptiness rather than connect with life. While these pursuits may temporarily soothe, they ultimately deplete energy and dull true joy.

Attachment and Dependency

Because the Sacral governs connection and intimacy, overactivity can manifest as emotional dependency or fear of being alone. The desire for closeness becomes possessive or overwhelming. In relationships, this may appear as clinging, jealousy, or using sensuality as a substitute for emotional safety.

Creative Chaos

An overcharged Svadhisthana can unleash intense bursts of creativity that lack focus or follow-through. Ideas multiply faster than they can be manifested, leading to frustration or exhaustion. The person may start many projects but finish few, mistaking constant activity for authentic creative flow.

Sensual Overload

Pleasure, when balanced, nourishes the soul. But when the Sacral Chakra is excessive, sensuality can become compulsive.

This may appear as an obsession with appearance, sexual escapism, or the pursuit of pleasure without emotional connection. The joy of union gives way to emptiness once the stimulation fades.

Loss of Emotional Boundaries

Overactive Sacral energy dissolves boundaries, making it difficult to separate one's emotions from others'. Empaths or highly sensitive individuals may absorb moods and desires from their surroundings, leaving them drained or confused about what truly belongs to them.

Physical Manifestations

Excess energy in the Sacral Chakra often shows up in the reproductive and lower abdominal region — such as hormonal imbalances, urinary irritation, menstrual pain, or addictive cycles tied to pleasure and release. The body may feel overstimulated, overheated, or restless.

The Hidden Lesson

Overactive Sacral energy teaches that freedom without balance becomes chaos. Just as a river needs its banks to flow with purpose, emotion and desire need the grounding of the Root to remain life-giving.

Healing begins not by denying passion but by containing it — learning that pleasure deepens through presence, not intensity. When emotional waters are held within safe boundaries, creativity and sensuality become sacred expressions rather than escapes.

The Experience of an Imbalanced Sacral

When the Sacral Chakra (Svadhisthana) is out of balance, life can feel like a tide that no longer follows the moon — sometimes frozen, sometimes flooding, never quite at ease. Because this chakra governs emotion, creativity, pleasure, and intimacy, its imbalance touches nearly every part of our human experience: how we feel, how we connect, how we create, and how we allow ourselves to receive joy.

An imbalanced Sacral Chakra often reveals itself in the subtle tension between control and surrender. You may feel too much or too little — overwhelmed by emotion or unable to feel at all. The waters of this chakra, once meant to flow with grace and vitality, become murky, stagnant, or stormy.

Emotional Signs

Emotionally, an imbalance at the Sacral often feels like instability. You may notice mood swings, sudden waves of sadness, or bursts of passion followed by guilt or fatigue. Feelings of shame, rejection, or creative frustration may arise, especially around intimacy or self-expression. When blocked, you may feel numb or emotionally distant; when overactive, emotions can spill over uncontrollably, leaving you drained.

Mental and Behavioral Signs

Mentally, imbalance may appear as self-doubt or confusion about what truly brings happiness. You might question your desires or judge yourself for wanting pleasure, affection, or rest. For some, it shows up as people-pleasing — trying to earn love instead of receiving it naturally. For others, it manifests as escapism: diving into fantasy, entertainment, or sensual excess to avoid deeper emotional truths.

Creative Symptoms

Because the Sacral Chakra is the center of creation — both artistic and biological — imbalance can block inspiration or scatter it. You may feel creatively dry, uninspired, or unable to complete projects. Or you may experience bursts of ideas that lack focus or structure. Creativity becomes inconsistent, dependent on emotional highs instead of a steady flow.

Relational Dynamics

In relationships, imbalance can cause patterns of dependency, fear of intimacy, or avoidance of vulnerability. When closed, the heart withdraws from connection; when overstimulated, it seeks validation through attention or affection. This push-pull dynamic creates emotional confusion — wanting closeness but fearing loss of self.

Physical Manifestations

On the physical level, the Sacral Chakra corresponds to the hips, pelvis, lower abdomen, and reproductive system. Imbalance can appear as menstrual irregularities, fertility challenges, sexual dysfunction, lower back pain, urinary or bladder issues, or tension in the hips. The body may literally hold emotional energy — tight, sore, or heavy where feelings have been stored instead of expressed.

The Inner Experience

Perhaps most deeply, an imbalanced Sacral Chakra feels like being cut off from life's rhythm — as if joy is always just out of reach. There is a longing to feel alive again, to trust pleasure without guilt, to express without fear. The lesson of Svadhisthana is that emotions and desires are not the enemy — they are messages from the soul, inviting us to reconnect with the flow of creation itself.

When the Sacral Chakra comes back into balance, life begins to move again.
Emotions become currents, not floods. Creativity awakens naturally.
Pleasure becomes sacred, and intimacy becomes safe.

Balance at Svadhisthana is not about control — it is about trust.
Trusting the body. Trusting emotion. Trusting the flow of life itself.

Chapter 5 – Causes of Disturbance

Childhood Instability and Trauma

If the Root Chakra is where we learn that life is safe, the Sacral Chakra is where we learn that life can be *felt*. It is here, in early childhood, that we first begin to explore emotion, pleasure, and connection — how we express affection, how we are comforted, and how we relate to others.

When these early experiences are nurturing, the Sacral energy develops fluidly. We learn that feelings are natural, that our emotions matter, and that joy, play, and creativity are welcome. But when instability, neglect, or emotional trauma arise, the natural flow of Svadhisthana becomes disrupted. The waters of emotion, once meant to move freely, are forced into stillness or turbulence.

Emotional Suppression and Shame

Many disturbances in the Sacral Chakra trace back to moments when a child's feelings or desires were dismissed, criticized, or punished. Phrases like "Don't cry," "Be quiet," or "That's not appropriate" teach children to shut down their emotional flow. Over time, this creates deep shame around expression — the belief that one's emotions are too much, too messy, or unworthy of love.

Loss of Emotional Attunement

When caregivers are emotionally unavailable, unpredictable, or overwhelmed, children lose the experience of attunement — the sense of being seen, heard, and mirrored. Without this, they struggle later in life to recognize or regulate their own emotions. The Sacral Chakra becomes either overactive (seeking constant validation and emotional connection) or underactive (numbing out and avoiding feeling).

Betrayal of Trust and Boundary Violations

Because Svadhisthana governs intimacy and boundaries, violations in these areas — whether emotional, physical, or sexual — create deep wounding. The body stores this memory, and the energy center closes down to protect the psyche. Later, this may appear as fear of touch, disconnection from sensuality, or difficulty trusting others in close relationships.

Emotional Role Reversal

In some homes, children are asked to meet the emotional needs of their parents — comforting them, keeping peace, or taking on adult responsibilities too soon. This reverses the natural flow of giving and receiving, leading to guilt around pleasure or self-care. The child learns that joy must be earned or that their feelings come second to others—the Sacral energy contracts in confusion between love and obligation.

Neglect of Joy and Play

The Sacral Chakra is the home of joy, curiosity, and imagination. When a child is not allowed to play, explore, or express freely — whether due to strict environments, fear-based control, or excessive pressure — creative energy dims. As adults, this can appear as creative block, chronic seriousness, or the inability to relax into pleasure without guilt.

The Lasting Impact

Childhood instability teaches the body that pleasure and emotion are unsafe. The adult may seek control to avoid vulnerability or chase intensity to feel alive again. Both patterns stem from the same wound — a disruption of emotional flow in the formative years.

Healing the Sacral Chakra involves gently re-teaching the body that it is safe to feel. Through creative play, mindful touch, and emotional expression, we begin to reopen the waters that were once dammed by fear or shame.

As the inner child learns that joy is not dangerous and emotion is not weakness, the Sacral Chakra begins to glow again — warm, fluid, and alive with creative possibility.

Poverty, Scarcity, and Emotional Deprivation

The Sacral Chakra (Svadhisthana) governs not only creativity and pleasure but also our capacity to *receive* — love, affection, attention, and emotional nourishment. When life feels emotionally or sensually barren, the result is not unlike material poverty at the Root level. A person may survive physically, yet feel starved inside.

Where the Root asks, *"Am I safe?"* the Sacral asks, *"Am I allowed to feel and enjoy?"* When that question goes unanswered, emotional scarcity takes hold, leaving the heart hungry for connection and joy.

Emotional Poverty

Emotional poverty arises when affection, comfort, or healthy emotional expression was withheld or inconsistent during formative years. This lack of warmth teaches the body to guard its feelings, suppress desires, or replace emotional intimacy with external achievements.

In adulthood, this may manifest as difficulty receiving love, fear of vulnerability, or reliance on validation to feel worthy. The person may appear independent yet feel an inner emptiness — a quiet ache for connection.

Scarcity of Pleasure and Joy

Just as financial scarcity creates fear of not having enough, emotional scarcity creates guilt or discomfort around pleasure. Those with an undernourished Sacral Chakra often struggle to relax, laugh, or enjoy life without justification. Pleasure feels indulgent, undeserved, or fleeting.

This deprivation can stem from cultural or familial beliefs that equate joy with laziness, sensuality with sin, or play with irresponsibility. Over time, such conditioning restricts the natural flow of pleasure energy — leaving the emotional body dry and brittle.

Survival Through Control

When emotional deprivation is prolonged, control becomes a substitute for safety. The person may manage relationships, emotions, or even creativity to avoid the risk of rejection or loss. Instead of allowing emotional flow, they build walls around the heart.

This survival strategy may provide short-term stability but long-term stagnation. The waters of Svadhisthana, meant to move freely, become contained and heavy — protecting from pain but also blocking joy.

Intergenerational Scarcity

Just as financial fears can be inherited, emotional scarcity is often passed down through generations. Families who endured hardship, repression, or trauma may unconsciously teach restraint over expression — silence instead of feeling. The result is an emotional lineage of "not enough" that continues until someone chooses to heal it.

Breaking this pattern means re-learning abundance on a feeling level: that there is enough love, enough joy, enough permission to feel fully alive.

Long-Term Effects

Living with emotional deprivation or pleasure scarcity can lead to:
• Difficulty forming or sustaining intimate relationships
• Feeling undeserving of love or affection
• Creative blockages and loss of inspiration
• Guilt around relaxation, rest, or sensual pleasure
• Emotional numbness or inability to access joy
• A tendency toward emotional overgiving or people-pleasing to earn connection

Healing the Energy of Emotional Scarcity

Healing the Sacral Chakra begins by gently reawakening the capacity to receive. It asks us to open the heart to life's sweetness again — through laughter, touch, movement, art, and affection.

Where the Root heals through grounding, the Sacral heals through *flow*.

Through small, consistent acts of pleasure — savoring a meal, dancing freely, creating art without judgment — the energy of abundance slowly returns.

The mantra becomes:
"There is enough love. There is enough joy. There is enough for me."

As emotional richness replaces deprivation, Svadhisthana transforms from a reservoir of longing into a river of creativity, connection, and genuine delight.

Ancestral Patterns of Fear, Migration, or Displacement

The Sacral Chakra does not only hold our personal emotions — it carries the emotional memories of those who came before us. Just as we inherit physical traits through DNA, we also inherit energetic patterns through the field of consciousness that connects family lines.

When our ancestors experienced emotional loss, separation, or forced displacement, those imprints can remain alive in the waters of Svadhisthana. These inherited emotions often surface as unexplained grief, difficulty forming deep bonds, or fear of abandonment — even when our present lives seem stable and secure.

Inherited Emotional Memory

The Sacral Chakra governs connection and belonging. When our ancestors endured war, exile, cultural loss, or migration, the natural rhythm of emotional security was disrupted. Their grief, longing, and sense of displacement often went unspoken — yet their descendants may still feel it as subtle unease or restlessness within.

You might carry feelings of sadness, instability, or nostalgia for "a home you've never known." This is the echo of emotional memory passed through generations — the body remembering what the mind cannot name.

Disrupted Bonds and Intimacy

Ancestral trauma can fracture the energetic blueprint of emotional connection. Families shaped by fear or survival may have learned to withhold affection, avoid vulnerability, or silence feelings to protect themselves. These patterns ripple through generations, teaching descendants to suppress emotion or equate intimacy with danger.

In the Sacral Chakra, this appears as difficulty trusting others, fear of loss, or cycles of emotional withdrawal and pursuit. Healing these patterns requires re-establishing trust — not only in others, but in the body's ability to feel safe again.

Cultural Displacement and Identity Loss

When a lineage is uprooted from its land, language, or traditions, a deeper disconnection occurs — not only from the earth (Root), but from *emotional identity* (Sacral). Creativity, ritual, and expression — all governed by Svadhisthana — become muted or forgotten.
You may feel disconnected from your cultural or creative roots, longing to rediscover a lost rhythm of belonging and expression.

Reclaiming ancestral art forms, music, storytelling, or ritual can reawaken the Sacral's flow. These acts reconnect you to the emotional wisdom your lineage once expressed through creation, song, and movement.

The Fear of Feeling Too Much

Families shaped by grief or trauma often pass down a silent rule: *"Do not feel too deeply."* This inherited caution against emotion leads descendants to guard their hearts, fearing that opening to feeling might reopen ancient wounds. Yet this very suppression keeps the Sacral waters stagnant.

Healing comes when we give ourselves permission to feel what our ancestors could not. Every tear, every dance, every act of creation becomes a thread of restoration — returning flow where it was once blocked by fear.

Healing Through Emotional Flow

To heal ancestral patterns within the Sacral Chakra:
• Acknowledge the stories and struggles of those who came before you.
• Engage in creative or ritual practices that honor your lineage.
• Use water ceremonies — baths, rivers, tears — to symbolically release inherited grief.
• Affirm: *"I honor what my ancestors endured, and I allow the emotions they could not express to flow through me and return to peace."*

The Deeper Lesson

Where the Root carries the inherited memory of survival, the Sacral carries the inherited memory of feeling. When generations could not afford to feel, the emotional body froze.

By reclaiming joy, sensuality, and creative freedom, you do more than heal yourself — you heal your lineage. The waters of Svadhisthana begin to move again, carrying forward not the pain of the past, but the living rhythm of renewal.

Environmental and Energetic Toxins: Violence, Stress, Societal Instability

The Sacral Chakra (Svadhisthana) is the emotional center of the human energy system — the part of us that feels the world. While the Root reacts to physical danger, the Sacral absorbs the energetic climate around us. It responds to every vibration of emotion, sound, and atmosphere, like water reflecting the sky above it. When the outer world is filled with violence, fear, or chaos, this chakra often bears the weight first.

The Sensitive Nature of Svadhisthana

The element of water makes the Sacral uniquely receptive. It thrives in environments of peace, creativity, and emotional honesty — yet it contracts in the presence of conflict, aggression, or suppression. Just as polluted water cannot nourish life, a toxic environment clouds this energy center, dulling joy, numbing creativity, and distorting emotional balance.

Every time we witness cruelty, experience stress, or absorb collective fear through media, community, or relationships, the Sacral registers it as a disturbance in emotional safety. The body may not always recognize the difference between *personal* and *collective* pain — both are felt in the same waters of being.

Exposure to Violence and Aggression

Whether experienced directly or indirectly, exposure to violence shakes the Sacral's sense of safety in relationships and the world. Even witnessing aggression — at home, in media, or in society — creates an undercurrent of fear that tightens the pelvic and abdominal region. Over time, this chronic tension can manifest as reproductive issues, bladder discomfort, or emotional detachment from intimacy and trust.

For sensitive individuals, these experiences can lead to emotional overload — a state where the psyche unconsciously suppresses feelings to avoid pain. Pleasure and passion diminish, replaced by guardedness or hypervigilance.

Chronic Stress and Overstimulation

Modern life subjects the Sacral Chakra to constant stress. The relentless pace of work, digital noise, and emotional pressure overstimulate this energy center.
Instead of flowing rhythmically like a tide, the Sacral begins to oscillate erratically — swinging between emotional numbness and overwhelm. The body struggles to regulate hormonal balance and emotional rhythms, leading to exhaustion, mood swings, and reduced creativity.

This imbalance often shows up as irritability, anxiety in relationships, loss of desire, or burnout in creative professions. The very energy meant for creation and connection becomes drained by the demands of survival in an overstimulated world.

Societal Instability and Collective Fear

The Sacral Chakra is also influenced by the emotional energy of the collective. Times of political unrest, environmental crisis, or economic uncertainty create a psychic "undertow" that many unconsciously absorb. Even those who are safe in their personal lives may feel uneasy, restless, or creatively blocked, reflecting the collective emotional waters of humanity.

This shared instability affects community bonding, trust, and the collective sense of pleasure and joy. When society itself feels unsafe, individuals unconsciously restrict their capacity to feel fully — as though emotional openness is a risk.

Energetic Contamination

Beyond the visible world, energetic toxins — such as environments filled with conflict, resentment, or unspoken tension — can drain the Sacral field. Because this chakra is relational, it picks up the energy of spaces and people easily. Emotional clutter, gossip, unresolved anger, or even electromagnetic overstimulation can muddy the Sacral aura, creating fatigue and confusion.

Clearing these influences through grounding, salt baths, sound healing, or creative expression helps the energy body "detox" and regain clarity.

Healing Through Emotional Cleanse

The antidote to energetic pollution is emotional purification — reconnecting with what feels true, soft, and alive.
• Limit exposure to violent media and overstimulating noise.
• Spend time near natural water — lakes, oceans, rivers, or even a warm bath — to harmonize your inner waters.
• Practice emotional hygiene: express feelings daily through journaling, art, dance, or tears.
• Surround yourself with beauty, calm, and supportive relationships.

The Deeper Lesson

The Sacral Chakra teaches that sensitivity is not weakness — it is wisdom.
To feel deeply in a chaotic world is to remain human.
But sensitivity requires boundaries. The path of Svadhisthana is to stay open enough to feel, yet strong enough to flow without absorbing every wave of pain around us.

When we cleanse our emotional waters, we reclaim the ability to feel without drowning — to create, to love, and to live with joy even in turbulent times.

Sexual Trauma, Repression, and Emotional Violation

The Sacral Chakra (Svadhisthana) is the seat of intimacy, sensuality, and emotional flow. It is where we experience the pleasure of being alive and the sacred exchange of energy through touch, connection, and trust.
When that trust is broken — through trauma, repression, or violation — the very core of Svadhisthana is shaken. Its natural rhythm of openness and flow contracts into fear, shame, or numbness.

Sexual trauma is one of the deepest wounds to this energy center, because it not only affects the body but also fractures the spirit's sense of safety within the body. Repression, too, can be a quieter form of trauma — one that teaches us that our natural sensuality is wrong, our emotions are dangerous, or our pleasure must be hidden.

Energetic Impact of Violation

When sexual or emotional boundaries are crossed, the Sacral Chakra closes instinctively to protect the psyche. The body stores the memory of invasion — not only in the mind, but in the tissues, muscles, and energetic field.
You may feel disconnected from your body, detached during intimacy, or fearful of being touched. Some experience the opposite: overidentifying with sensuality as a way to reclaim power, while still feeling emotionally unfulfilled.

Both responses — withdrawal or overexposure — stem from the same wound: a lost sense of safety in one's own body.

The Legacy of Shame

In many cultures, shame is used to control emotion and sexuality. From an early age, people are taught that pleasure is sinful, desire is dangerous, and the body must be hidden or denied.
This collective repression distorts the Sacral energy field, replacing natural curiosity and joy with guilt and secrecy. Even without direct trauma, the internalized belief that sensuality is "wrong" can be enough to silence the Sacral's voice and cut off emotional flow.

Shame is a heavy vibration — it sinks into the waters of Svadhisthana like sediment, clouding vitality and creative inspiration.

Emotional Violation Beyond the Physical

Not all Sacral wounding is physical. Emotional betrayal, manipulation, coercion, or neglect can also scar this energy center. When trust is broken or emotional vulnerability is exploited, the same energetic response occurs: contraction, withdrawal, and loss of creative or sensual confidence.

These experiences can lead to difficulty expressing needs, fear of intimacy, or feeling "too much" or "not enough" in relationships. The Sacral learns to associate closeness with pain, and so it suppresses its natural fluidity to stay safe.

Physical Manifestations

Because the Sacral governs the reproductive system, trauma or repression can manifest as pelvic pain, irregular cycles, low libido, infertility, urinary issues, or tightness in the hips. The body holds emotional tension in these regions — a silent guarding of the past.

Often, healing begins not through words but through movement, touch, and breath — gentle ways of teaching the body that it is once again safe to inhabit.

Pathways to Healing

Healing the Sacral after trauma or repression is an act of reclaiming ownership of your body, emotions, and pleasure. This journey is deeply personal and often unfolds slowly, in layers of trust.

Key approaches include:

• **Safety First:** Ground healing in the Root Chakra — rebuild safety in the body before exploring pleasure.

• **Gentle Reconnection:** Use mindful movement, yoga, or somatic therapy to awaken the hips and reconnect to sensation.

• **Creative Expression:** Art, dance, and journaling allow emotions to move without words. Creativity is the Sacral's native language.

• **Compassionate Witnessing:** Work with trusted practitioners, therapists, or healers who hold space for your process without judgment.

• **Affirmations of Innocence:** Replace inherited or imposed shame with truth — *"My body is sacred. My emotions are natural. Pleasure is my birthright."*

The Deeper Lesson

Sexual and emotional trauma reveal how deeply the human spirit longs for safety, respect, and love. The Sacral Chakra does not heal by erasing the past, but by transforming the energy of pain into the wisdom of compassion.

Each time you reclaim a piece of your sensual joy or creative spark, you are not only healing yourself — you are rewriting the collective story of shame into one of sacred embodiment.

To feel pleasure again after pain is an act of profound courage. It is to say: *I am still here. I am still whole. I am worthy of love, trust, and joy.*

Chapter 6 – Signs of Balance

Emotional Flow: Pleasure, Creativity, and Connection

When the Sacral Chakra (Svadhisthana) is balanced, life feels vibrant, sensual, and creatively alive. The emotional body moves freely — not trapped in numbness or chaos, but flowing with grace and responsiveness. Just as the moon guides the tides, the balanced Sacral guides the rhythm of our feelings, desires, and relationships.

Svadhisthana in harmony brings joy in embodiment — the ability to feel, create, and connect without fear or guilt. It invites a deep sense of intimacy with life itself.

Pleasure

Pleasure is the first and most essential gift of a balanced Sacral Chakra. It is not indulgence, but the natural joy of being alive. You find delight in small moments — the warmth of sunlight, laughter with a friend, the taste of food, or the rhythm of movement.

Balanced pleasure is mindful and nourishing. It arises from presence, not from escape. When Svadhisthana flows freely, you give yourself permission to enjoy life without shame. The senses awaken, reminding you that the body is not an obstacle to spirituality but its sacred vessel.

Creativity

The Sacral Chakra is the womb of creation — where imagination takes form. When in balance, creativity emerges naturally and joyfully. Ideas flow with ease; inspiration feels abundant and unforced.

You express yourself through art, words, music, movement, or simply the way you live. Creativity becomes a spiritual act — the soul expressing its beauty through form. In this state, there is no need for perfection; creation itself becomes an offering to life.

Connection

The balanced Sacral allows for emotional depth and intimacy. You can both give and receive affection without losing yourself. Relationships feel fluid and authentic — neither clinging nor avoiding, but moving with natural reciprocity.

Empathy deepens as you become more attuned to your own feelings and those of others. This emotional intelligence creates harmony in communication, collaboration, and love.

Emotional Balance

In a balanced Svadhisthana, emotions flow like clear water — they move through you, rather than overwhelm or stagnate. You can feel sadness without drowning in it, anger without destroying, and joy without grasping.

This emotional maturity brings inner peace and resilience. Life's changes are met with grace rather than resistance. You trust the ebb and flow of experience, knowing that no emotion defines you — all are waves returning to the same ocean of awareness.

Healthy Sensuality

Balanced Sacral energy restores the sacredness of sensuality. Sexuality becomes an expression of love, creativity, and divine union — not a source of shame or control. The body feels safe and alive, and pleasure becomes a prayer of gratitude.

This energy radiates outward as confidence, magnetism, and authenticity. You no longer seek validation through desire, but share intimacy as a reflection of self-love and wholeness.

The Feeling of Emotional Flow

Together, pleasure, creativity, and connection create a sense of *emotional abundance.* This is the opposite of repression or excess. The balanced Sacral flows in harmony — open but contained, expressive yet centered.

In this state, you feel at home in your emotions, comfortable in your body, and inspired by life itself. Joy, affection, and creativity become natural extensions of your being.

To live with a balanced Sacral Chakra is to live in rhythm with the tides of life — open, responsive, and beautifully human.

Physical Vitality: Reproductive System, Lower Abdomen, and Water Element

The Sacral Chakra governs the realm of creation — both biological and creative. When Svadhisthana is balanced, the body's fluid systems flow with ease, vitality, and sensitivity. This includes the reproductive organs, kidneys, bladder, and lower abdomen. As the Root provides structure, the Sacral provides movement — it is the river that animates the body with vitality and sensuality.

Reproductive System: The Womb of Life

The reproductive organs — uterus, ovaries, testes, and pelvic region — are the physical home of the Sacral Chakra. When energy here is balanced, vitality, fertility, and sensuality are harmonious. You feel comfortable with your sexuality and see it as sacred rather than shameful.
This doesn't only refer to biological creation, but to the creative spark in every human — the ability to give birth to ideas, projects, and dreams.

Lower Abdomen: The Seat of Flow

The lower abdomen is the physical container of emotional and creative energy. When this area feels open and relaxed, emotions flow naturally and digestion is strong — you "digest" life experience with ease. Tension, cramping, or stagnation often point to emotional holding or suppressed expression. Balanced Sacral energy allows this area to feel warm, supple, and alive — the center of inner rhythm.

Kidneys and Bladder: The Regulators of Flow

Linked to the water element, the kidneys and bladder symbolize purification, balance, and release. They regulate not just physical fluids but emotional flow. When you allow emotions to move through you rather than resist them, this system functions optimally. When emotions are repressed, stagnation or imbalance may appear in these organs.

The Element of Water

Water is the essence of Svadhisthana — adaptive, cleansing, and creative. When balanced, water energy teaches us to move with life rather than against it. It allows us to adapt to change, release resistance, and express emotions fluidly.

The Feeling of Physical Flow

A balanced Sacral Chakra brings a sense of *fluid vitality*. The body feels graceful, sensual, and expressive. Movement becomes pleasure rather than effort; energy feels abundant but calm. The body becomes a vessel for creative and emotional flow, carrying the rhythms of life with ease.

Spiritual Qualities: Creativity, Sensuality, and Sacred Relationship

When Svadhisthana is balanced, spirituality becomes embodied — not something distant or abstract, but something you *feel* moving through you. The Sacral teaches that divine energy flows not only in temples or meditation halls but also in art, dance, intimacy, and joy.

Creativity as Divine Expression

The Sacral Chakra reveals that creativity is a form of worship — the soul expressing itself through form. Whether through painting, music, cooking, or problem-solving, creation becomes a dialogue between self and the universe. You begin to understand that inspiration is divine flow moving through your human vessel.

Sensuality as Sacred Awareness

Balanced sensuality is not lust or indulgence; it is presence. It is the ability to feel life fully — the touch of wind, the rhythm of breath, the pulse of your heartbeat. In this awareness, the senses become sacred instruments of connection between spirit and body.

Intimacy and Emotional Trust

A balanced Sacral awakens the spiritual truth of emotional intimacy: vulnerability is not weakness but courage. You can open your heart without fear of losing yourself, because you trust the flow of giving and receiving. Relationships become spaces of creative exchange, not control.

Connection to the Flow of Life

Spiritually, the Sacral teaches surrender — the art of trusting life's rhythm. Just as rivers carve their path effortlessly toward the ocean, you learn that your emotional and creative flows are part of a larger movement of divine intelligence.

The Experience of a Balanced Sacral Chakra

When the Sacral Chakra is in harmony, life feels fluid and inspired. Emotions move freely, creativity blossoms, and relationships deepen with authenticity. The body feels alive, responsive, and sensual — not in excess, but in balance.

Physical Experience

The lower abdomen feels open and relaxed. Movement is graceful and pleasurable. Reproductive health, hormonal balance, and vitality are stable. You feel comfortable in your body, celebrating its rhythms rather than resisting them.

Emotional Experience

Emotions flow easily without suppression or overwhelm. Joy, passion, and empathy arise naturally. You can feel deeply without losing your center and recover quickly from emotional waves.

Mental Experience

The mind of a balanced Sacral is imaginative and fluid. Ideas emerge with ease, and creativity feels effortless. You can think symbolically, dream vividly, and solve problems intuitively.

Spiritual Experience

Spiritually, you feel connected to the divine flow that animates all creation. Life feels like a dance — one of rhythm, beauty, and sacred relationship. The separation between the physical and spiritual dissolves, and every act of creation becomes an act of devotion.

Overall Experience

To live with a balanced Sacral Chakra is to live in harmony with the tides of life — emotionally open, sensually alive, and creatively abundant. You trust in the flow, knowing that pleasure and purpose are not opposites but partners in your sacred journey.

Chapter 7 – Hidden Secrets & Esoteric Wisdom

Tantra and the Sacral Chakra

In the Tantric view, **Svadhisthana** is the chamber where Kundalini begins to stir. If the Root Chakra represents grounding and the first ignition of life, the Sacral Chakra represents movement — the awakening of emotion, creativity, and the sensual pulse of existence. It is the place where spirit learns to flow through form.

Just as Muladhara anchors consciousness into matter, Svadhisthana teaches that once grounded, energy must *move*. Tantra describes this as the sacred dance of Shakti — the divine feminine current — beginning her ascent through the spine. When Kundalini energy awakens, she first rises through the Root's foundation and begins to swirl and spiral through the waters of the Sacral.

Kundalini Awakening Through the Lower Chakras

Kundalini's journey begins with **the opening of the Heart**, for the heart's devotion and purity guide the safe awakening of energy. From there, awareness descends to the **Root**, where grounding and stability are cultivated — creating the vessel strong enough to hold rising power. Only then can Kundalini begin her first true movement within **the Sacral Chakra**, the womb of creation.

Here, energy becomes fluid, sensual, and emotionally expressive. The sacred serpent that once slept in Muladhara now begins to uncoil and undulate, creating the rhythmic flow that will one day carry her to the crown. The Sacral Chakra marks this transition from stillness to motion, from survival to creation, from existence to experience.

The Sacred Water of Life

In Tantra, **Svadhisthana** is governed by the element of water — symbolizing emotion, pleasure, and flow. Water has no resistance; it finds its path through softness, adaptability, and rhythm. When Kundalini begins to move here, she teaches surrender — the art of allowing rather than controlling.

This is where emotion becomes energy in motion. The ancient texts describe the Sacral as a **sacred river** within the subtle body, flowing between the Root (earth) and the Solar Plexus (fire). It is through this river that creativity, sensuality, and the capacity for connection are born.

The Body as a Sacred Vessel

Tantra views the body not as an obstacle but as the temple of awakening. The Sacral Chakra, located near the reproductive organs, is revered as the *yoni-sthana* — the creative seat of Shakti herself. Sexual energy here is not sinful or profane; it is divine life force, capable of birthing worlds both physical and spiritual.

When honored consciously, this energy becomes **Ojas**, refined spiritual vitality. When suppressed or misused, it becomes **Apana**, draining vitality downward. Tantric practice transforms desire into devotion — reminding us that pleasure, creation, and spiritual ecstasy all flow from the same divine source.

The Polarity of Shakti and Shiva in Motion

While Muladhara represents the resting Shakti — grounded, still, and coiled — Svadhisthana represents Shakti in motion. Here, her dance begins. The divine feminine awakens not in opposition to Shiva, but in sacred play with him. Shiva, pure consciousness, witnesses her movement; Shakti, pure energy, creates form.

This polarity generates the cosmic rhythm of life itself — expansion and contraction, flow and containment, feeling and awareness. Through Svadhisthana, Tantra reveals that all emotion and sensuality are sacred when infused with consciousness.

Tantric Practices for the Sacral Chakra

Traditional Tantric methods to awaken and harmonize Svadhisthana include:

- **Bija Mantra:** Chanting *VAM*, the seed sound of the Sacral, to awaken creative and emotional flow.
- **Yantra Meditation:** Visualizing the crescent moon resting in water — the symbol of Svadhisthana — to balance emotion and intuition.
- **Breathwork:** Pelvic breathing or wave breathing, allowing the inhale to rise from the hips and the exhale to ripple downward, awakening the inner tide.
- **Sacred Movement:** Dance, gentle yoga, or flowing gestures that allow Shakti to express through the body.
- **Ritual and Sensual Awareness:** Honoring the senses — sight, touch, sound, taste, and scent — as pathways to divine experience rather than distractions from it.

The Secret Wisdom of the Sacral

The hidden Tantric teaching of Svadhisthana is that **pleasure is sacred when it is conscious**. It is not indulgence but reverence — an acknowledgment that joy and creation are divine rights of embodiment.

Where the Root taught grounding and survival, the Sacral teaches surrender and flow.
Where the Root taught "I exist," the Sacral whispers, "I feel, I create, I connect."

Kundalini's awakening here reminds us that the path to enlightenment is not an escape from emotion or desire but their *transmutation*. The same force that births a child, paints a masterpiece, or stirs passion in the heart is the power that leads the soul toward divine union.

In the language of Tantra, the Sacral Chakra is not merely the center of pleasure — it is the **womb of awakening**, the sacred water through which Shakti begins her ascent toward the infinite.

Kundalini: Awakening Through the Waters of the Sacral Chakra

The Serpent Stirs

At the Root, Kundalini lies coiled in stillness — silent, potent, and waiting.
When consciousness descends through the heart and anchors safely in the Root, the sacred serpent begins to stir. Her first movements are subtle — a warmth in the pelvis, a wave of emotion, a quiet awakening of desire or creativity. This is the

whisper of Shakti, reminding the soul that it is meant not only to survive, but to *feel*.

As energy flows upward into the Sacral Chakra, the still earth of Muladhara meets the moving waters of Svadhisthana. The dormant fire of life transforms into a living current — rippling, sensual, and alive. Emotion begins to awaken as divine intelligence; pleasure becomes prayer. The body remembers itself as sacred.

Here, Shakti's dance begins — not in chaos, but in rhythm. She undulates through the waters of the Sacral, teaching that flow is not weakness but wisdom, and that feeling is the language through which the soul learns to move.

Signs of Awakening

As Kundalini moves through the Sacral Chakra, each person experiences her in unique ways. The sensations may be delicate or profound, physical or emotional, but they all carry the signature of awakening life force.

You may notice:

- A gentle pulsing, tingling, or warmth in the lower abdomen or pelvis
- A rise in emotional sensitivity — feeling inspired, moved, or tender
- Spontaneous creativity, art, or expression seeking release
- Heightened sensuality or awareness of the body as energy
- Periods of emotional cleansing — tears, laughter, or waves of release

This is Shakti purifying the emotional body. The energy does not rush; it *flows*. It releases what has been suppressed, turning stagnant waters into a living current. When you allow this process with awareness, the Sacral becomes a temple — a space where emotion, pleasure, and spirit merge into devotion.

Balancing the Waters

Like a river that needs its banks to flow, Kundalini requires both grounding and containment. Too much movement without structure can lead to emotional flooding or loss of center; too much control, and the waters become stagnant.

The practice is balanced — allowing flow without drowning in it.

- When the Root remains strong, the waters of the Sacral move in harmony.
- When the Heart remains open, emotion transforms into compassion rather than chaos.

Tantra teaches: *"To feel fully is divine; to remain aware while feeling is mastery."*
Through breath, movement, and awareness, you learn to let emotion move *through* you, not *over* you. The energy that once fueled craving or fear becomes creative fire — a living current that nourishes body, heart, and soul alike.

Tantric Secrets of the Creative Fire

The Element of Water and the Fire Beneath It

The Sacral Chakra is the realm of water — fluid, emotional, and ever-changing. Yet beneath its shimmering surface lies a hidden fire: the creative spark that gives warmth, direction, and purpose to flow.

Water teaches surrender; fire teaches transformation. Together, they reveal the sacred balance between feeling and power, between emotion that moves and energy that creates.

When Kundalini enters Svadhisthana, the stillness of the Root becomes rhythm. The sacred waters begin to stir, heated by the inner flame of Shakti's awakening. Old emotions dissolve, creativity ignites, and vitality begins to shimmer through the body like sunlight rippling across water.

Pleasure as Prayer

In Tantra, pleasure is not indulgence — it is remembrance. It is the body's way of recognizing itself as divine.

Every sensation, every breath, every moment of joy is a form of worship when met with awareness. To feel deeply is to say yes to life; to experience pleasure consciously is to touch the divine in form.

When we repress pleasure, we dam the sacred river. When we chase it without presence, we lose its sanctity. But when we honor it — with gratitude, breath, and reverence — pleasure becomes prayer. It refines desire into devotion, turning ordinary experience into a sacred offering of life itself.

The Inner Marriage of Shiva and Shakti

At the heart of the Sacral Chakra lies the eternal dance of Shiva and Shakti — consciousness and energy, stillness and movement, awareness and emotion.

Shiva is the silent witness within; Shakti is the flowing pulse of life. When they unite in harmony, the result is creation — not only of life or art, but of balance, presence, and joy.

This union is the true *Sacred Marriage* — not between two lovers, but within oneself. When awareness (Shiva) embraces emotion (Shakti), every experience becomes sacred.

In this inner marriage, the fire beneath the waters burns steadily, warming but never consuming. The self becomes both the ocean and the flame, both the dancer and the dance.

Here, Tantra reveals its deepest secret:
Awakening is not an escape from life's sensations — it is the full, conscious embrace of them.

Kundalini and the Alchemy of Emotion

Emotion is the alchemy of the soul.
It is how the infinite speaks through the finite — the current of life expressing itself through feeling, movement, and rhythm. In the Sacral Chakra, Kundalini begins her true work of transformation: turning raw emotion into refined awareness, and desire into creative devotion.

Emotion as Energy in Motion

When Kundalini awakens in Svadhisthana, emotion becomes alive again. You may feel tides rising and falling within — waves of joy, tears of release, surges of passion, or moments of deep stillness.
This is the sacred current of Shakti moving through the waters of your being, clearing stagnation and restoring flow.

Tantric sages taught: *"To feel deeply is to begin awakening."*
Emotion is not weakness — it is movement. Each feeling, when met with awareness, becomes energy in motion — the language of Kundalini flowing through the body.

The Waters of Transformation

Water, the element of the Sacral, cleanses and purifies. When Kundalini rises here, she stirs the emotional body like a river after long stillness, bringing to the surface what was buried: grief, guilt, shame, longing, or forgotten joy.

This process is not punishment; it is purification.
The sacred waters dissolve the silt of suppression so the current can run clear again. Through each wave of emotion, the soul remembers how to flow.

Healing occurs not by escaping feeling, but by surrendering to its rhythm — by allowing emotion to move until it finds its still point within.

From Reaction to Creation

At the lower vibration of the Sacral, emotion expresses as reaction — instinctive and unconscious. But as Kundalini rises, awareness meets feeling, and a higher alchemy unfolds.

Anger refines into clarity.
Sadness softens into compassion.
Desire expands into creation.

This is the transformation of emotion into art — the process through which pain becomes purpose, and longing becomes light. The waters of Svadhisthana teach us to channel feeling rather than resist it, to let energy move through us as inspiration instead of imbalance.

The Dance of Shakti

When emotion flows freely, the body becomes a vessel of divine movement. Breath deepens, hips loosen, and subtle waves of energy begin to pulse from the pelvis through the spine. This is Shakti's dance — spontaneous, fluid, and alive.

There is no control here, only surrender. You become both dancer and witness, movement and stillness.
Pleasure becomes prayer. Expression becomes meditation.
Through this sacred dance, Shakti releases what the mind cannot, reminding you that healing happens not through thought, but through flow.

The Gold Within the Waters

Every emotion carries wisdom. Beneath the surface turbulence lies a golden essence — the lesson, the gift, the clarity.

When you sit with your emotions instead of suppressing or chasing them, they reveal their secret alchemy:

- Fear becomes awareness.
- Anger becomes direction.
- Grief becomes tenderness.
- Desire becomes creation.

Through this transmutation, the waters of the Sacral become luminous — no longer murky with the past, but clear, alive, and reflective of the soul's light.

The Hidden Tantric Truth

Kundalini does not rise *because* we feel less — she rises *because* we feel fully.
When emotion is honored rather than feared, the body becomes a sacred vessel.
When desire is seen as a divine impulse rather than sin, creation becomes worship.

In the alchemy of the Sacral, Shakti teaches that every tear, every sigh, every pulse of pleasure is part of the divine current awakening within you.
To feel deeply is not to fall — it is to flow toward the divine.
To create, to love, to move — these are the ways Kundalini rises through the waters, carrying you home to yourself.

Secret Uses of the Sacral: Lunar Mysteries, Creative Trance, and Emotional Alchemy

Beyond its association with sensuality and creativity, the Sacral Chakra conceals ancient wisdom about transformation through feeling, rhythm, and ritual.
Across traditions, this watery center was revered not just for pleasure, but for its power to bridge worlds — emotion and spirit, body and soul, human and divine.

Lunar Mysteries: The Moon Within

In Tantric and esoteric teachings, Svadhisthana is governed by the moon. The waxing and waning of lunar light mirrors the ebb and flow of our emotions, creativity, and sensual energy.
Ancient initiates used moon cycles to awaken their inner waters — meditating or performing rituals during new and full moons to harmonize their emotional tides with cosmic rhythms.

To work with the Sacral is to remember the art of timing — knowing when to create, when to release, when to rest, and when to rise again.
This lunar awareness aligns your emotions with nature's pulse, teaching that fluidity is not weakness, but wisdom.

Creative Trance and the Flow State

Artists, dancers, and mystics have long known the secret
doorway of Svadhisthana: the *flow state* — that moment when
time dissolves, and creation moves effortlessly through you.
In ancient temples, this was not seen as inspiration alone, but as
possession by the divine — Shakti herself moving through the
body of the devotee.

Drumming, chanting, movement, or rhythmic breath could all
activate this trance. As the mind quiets, awareness slips beneath
thought and into rhythm — the same pulse that beats within
ocean waves, heartbeats, and the womb's tide.
In this creative trance, individuality softens, and you become
the instrument of universal expression.

Emotional Alchemy: Turning Feeling into Power

Just as the alchemist turns lead into gold, the practitioner of
Svadhisthana turns raw emotion into creative energy.
Each feeling becomes material for transformation. Anger fuels
change. Sadness opens compassion. Desire becomes the
impulse to create beauty or connection.

Tantric adepts understood that emotion is not to be escaped but
refined.
Through conscious breath and movement, emotional energy can
be circulated upward through the chakras — feeding the heart
with empathy and the mind with inspiration.

This is the secret of the *sacral alchemist*: nothing within you is
wasted. Every feeling, once embraced, becomes fuel for
awakening.

Water Bonding: Reclaiming Flow

Just as the Root's sacred act was earth bonding, the Sacral's practice is *water bonding* — the art of communion with rivers, rain, and the ocean.
Immersing oneself in water resets the nervous system and restores emotional rhythm.
In many cultures, sacred bathing, moonlit swimming, or ritual cleansing marked the passage into new phases of life — symbolic baptisms into emotional renewal.

Spiritually, water bonding reconnects us to the fluid intelligence of life itself. It teaches release — how to let go of what no longer serves, and how to trust that every wave returns to the sea.

Primal Creativity

Where the Root's primal energy is expressed as survival, the Sacral's primal energy is expressed as creation.
This is not limited to reproduction but includes the entire spectrum of creative force — art, song, relationship, innovation, and expression.
In Tantra, this current is known as *Kama Shakti* — the creative eros of the cosmos. When channeled consciously, it fuels spiritual evolution as much as physical creation.

To access this force is to reclaim your birthright as a co-creator with the divine. The same energy that stirs the oceans moves your breath and births your dreams.

The Hidden Wisdom

The secret uses of the Sacral Chakra reveal it as far more than a center of pleasure. It is a portal of transformation — through emotion, rhythm, and creation.

Just as the Root connects us to earth, the Sacral connects us to the living waters of consciousness.

To honor Svadhisthana is to reclaim your inner tides — to remember that emotion is holy, creativity is divine, and flow is the natural language of life.

When you align with this current, you no longer fight your feelings — you sail them toward awakening.

Western Mysticism: The Waters of Creation and the Temple of Emotion

In Western mystical and esoteric traditions, water has always symbolized birth, purification, emotion, and divine creation. Just as the Root corresponds to earth — the foundation stone — the Sacral corresponds to water — the living current flowing through that temple. These teachings remind us that spirit does not only dwell in stillness but also in movement, rhythm, and feeling.

The Waters of Genesis

In the book of Genesis, creation begins not with form but with water:

"The Spirit of God moved upon the face of the waters."

This primordial sea represents potential — the unshaped essence from which all life emerges. In the language of energy, it is Svadhisthana before awakening — fertile, fluid, waiting for divine breath to stir its surface.
Western mystics interpreted these waters as the soul's emotional field — vast, creative, and capable of reflecting divine light when calm or distorting it when stirred by turmoil.

To work with the Sacral, then, is to return to those first waters of creation and learn to let Spirit move through emotion consciously.

The Temple of Emotion

While the Root builds the temple's foundation, the Sacral fills it with life — the flowing fountains, sacred oils, and anointing waters that make the temple a place of feeling and renewal. Medieval mystics often described divine experience as *"liquid love"* — a warmth that flows through the body and soul.
In Christian mysticism, baptism symbolizes this same transformation: the washing away of the old self to emerge reborn, cleansed, and emotionally awakened to divine grace.
In Kabbalistic tradition, the sefirah *Yesod* ("Foundation") mirrors the Sacral Chakra's role. It channels the creative energy of the higher spheres into manifestation, functioning as the bridge between vision and form. Yesod is lunar, reflective, and fluid — the sacred pool through which divine intention takes shape.

Alchemy and the Element of Water

In alchemy, water represents *solve* — dissolution, the process by which form softens so transformation can occur. The alchemist must first dissolve the fixed to make way for the new — just as emotion must flow before creativity or healing can emerge.
The alchemical symbol of the *Mercurial Waters* echoes Svadhisthana's essence: a substance both spiritual and physical, capable of reflecting and transmitting divine consciousness. When the inner waters stagnate, transformation halts; when they flow, consciousness refines itself into new awareness. Thus, alchemy teaches what Tantra already knew: emotion is not the obstacle to enlightenment — it is the medium of it.

Mysteries of the Moon and the Feminine Current

Western esoteric schools long revered the moon as the symbol of the Divine Feminine — intuitive, receptive, and cyclical. Goddesses such as Isis, Mary, and Sophia each embody the wisdom of water — the ability to hold, to gestate, and to reflect. Their stories remind us that creation requires both flow and containment, passion and patience.

In the mystical marriage of Christ and Sophia, or in the Hermetic union of Sol and Luna, the same polarity appears as in Tantra's Shiva and Shakti — consciousness and energy, spirit and form, merging through love.

This lunar current corresponds directly with the Sacral Chakra, teaching that divine creation is not a singular act but a rhythm — waxing and waning, ebbing and flowing, eternally renewing itself.

The Shared Wisdom

Across Western mysticism, the message mirrors that of the East: water is sacred because it *feels*.

Emotion, like the tides, connects all life. Creation is not born from logic alone but from the womb of the heart — from feeling infused with consciousness.

Whether through baptismal rites, alchemical dissolutions, or moonlit devotion to the Divine Feminine, Western traditions point to the same truth that Tantra sings through Svadhisthana:

The sacred waters of the soul are the pathways of divine creation.

When emotion flows freely, God moves through you.

Chapter 8 – Balancing & Healing Practices

Reiki Positions and Energy Protocols for the Sacral Chakra

The Sacral Chakra governs emotion, creativity, sensuality, and the capacity for flow. In Reiki and other energy modalities, Svadhisthana is often treated after the Root — once safety is established — to help energy move freely through the emotional and reproductive centers. Balancing this chakra restores joy, intimacy, and the ability to feel life deeply without fear or repression.

Hand Positions for the Sacral Chakra

Reiki hand placements for the Sacral Chakra are generally located around the lower abdomen, pelvis, and lower back — the region connected to the reproductive organs and emotional center. Practitioners should always ensure comfort, privacy, and consent, as this area holds deep vulnerability and sensitivity.

- **Lower Abdomen:** Hands placed just below the navel (hovering or lightly resting) help activate creativity, pleasure, and emotional balance.
- **Pelvis or Hips:** Positioning hands over the pelvic bones harmonizes reproductive and creative energy, balancing masculine and feminine polarity.
- **Lower Back (Sacrum):** Placing hands over the sacrum supports the release of emotional blockages and

awakens the flow of Kundalini energy in a gentle, grounded way.

- **Hips and Lower Abdomen Together:** One hand at the sacrum and one on the lower belly balances the front and back energy currents of Svadhisthana — containment and expression.

Energy Protocols

1. **Opening the Waters:**
   Begin by inviting Reiki to flow like warm water through the lower abdomen. This helps the client relax, release emotional tension, and reconnect to their natural rhythm.
2. **Restoring Flow:**
   Move between the front and back of the body — from the lower abdomen to the sacrum — to encourage circulation of energy through the pelvic bowl. This balances yin and yang, receptivity and action, helping emotions move without overwhelm.
3. **Releasing Emotional Residue:**
   The Sacral Chakra often stores unprocessed feelings — grief, guilt, shame, or fear of pleasure. Holding the hands at the sacrum allows Reiki to dissolve this emotional sediment gently, bringing lightness and clarity.
4. **Balancing the Waters:**
   Visualize the energy as a calm orange glow spreading through the pelvis and hips. Let it expand and stabilize, soft but contained — like a serene lake reflecting sunlight.
5. **Sealing the Flow:**
   To conclude, place your hands on the lower abdomen or hips, setting the intention for the energy to remain balanced. This helps clients integrate the emotional and creative release with grounded awareness.

Symbolic Support

Advanced Reiki practitioners may call upon symbols to deepen the healing:

- **Sei He Ki (Harmony Symbol):** Balances emotional energy and releases subconscious blocks tied to relationships, sexuality, and shame.
- **Cho Ku Rei (Power Symbol):** Strengthens the flow of life force, enhancing creative vitality and sensual awareness.
- **Dai Ko Myo (Master Symbol):** Invokes the higher essence of Shakti energy — transforming desire into devotion, and pleasure into sacred connection.

The Practitioner's Role

Working with the Sacral Chakra requires compassion, neutrality, and respect. Because this center governs intimacy and emotional trust, the practitioner's energetic presence must embody gentleness and integrity. A calm, accepting field allows clients to feel safe enough to let emotions rise and release naturally.

Reiki for Svadhisthana is not about control — it is about allowing. The practitioner becomes a vessel through which energy remembers how to flow again, transforming stagnation into vitality and repression into creative freedom.

Healing Reminder

Reiki at the Sacral Chakra teaches one of the most profound spiritual truths:
Flow is healing. Emotion is sacred. Pleasure is divine.

As the waters of Svadhisthana are restored, life begins to move again — gently, rhythmically, and joyfully.
Through this flow, the soul remembers:

"I am free to feel. I am free to create. I am free to be."

Bridging the Root Chakra to the Heart Chakra

The chakras are not separate wheels turning in isolation — they form a living continuum of consciousness. Energy flows upward and downward through the body like a current, each center influencing the next. Among these connections, the passage from the Root (Muladhara) to the Heart (Anahata) — through the Sacral (Svadhisthana) — is one of the most profound.

It is the journey from survival to love, from instinct to emotion, and from fear to trust.

The Path from Root to Heart

Each chakra along this path refines the raw energy of life into greater awareness and connection:

- **Root (Muladhara):** Establishes safety, stability, and belonging — the foundation that anchors all other experiences.
- **Sacral (Svadhisthana):** Awakens emotion, pleasure, and creativity — transforming survival into expression, and grounding into flow.
- **Solar Plexus (Manipura):** Builds confidence, identity, and empowered action — giving shape and direction to the creative force of the Sacral.

- **Heart (Anahata):** Opens to love, compassion, and unity — allowing energy to transcend individuality and merge into divine connection.

When the energy moves clearly through these centers, the emotional waters of the Sacral serve as the *bridge of transformation* — carrying the grounded trust of the Root upward and infusing it with the warmth of the Heart.

The Role of the Sacral Chakra in the Bridge

Svadhisthana is the emotional translator between matter and spirit. It gives feeling to grounding and movement to love. Without the flow of emotion, the journey from safety to compassion cannot occur — love becomes abstract, unrooted in the body.

A healthy Sacral Chakra allows us to:

- Feel safe enough (Root) to express and connect.
- Experience pleasure and vulnerability as sacred acts of trust.
- Allow emotion to rise, purify, and soften the heart.

When blocked, energy may stagnate between Root and Heart — causing emotional numbness, guilt around pleasure, or difficulty giving and receiving love.
When open, the Sacral becomes the river that carries earth's stability upward into the heart's expansion.

The Energetic Ascent: From Fear to Love

The Root Chakra teaches: *"I am safe."*
The Sacral teaches: *"I feel."*
The Solar Plexus declares: *"I am."*
And the Heart reveals: *"I love."*

Each statement builds upon the one before it. Without safety, feeling cannot flow. Without feeling, identity becomes rigid. Without identity, love cannot open authentically.
The Sacral Chakra, then, is not merely a step along the way — it is the emotional alchemy that turns fear into trust and instinct into intimacy.

Living the Bridge

To bridge Root and Heart through the Sacral is to embody love in motion. It means being grounded enough to feel deeply and open enough to express those feelings with grace.
It is the practice of letting emotion rise like water — washing through the body, softening the mind, and nourishing the heart.

When the Root is stable, the Sacral flowing, and the Heart open, you become a conduit of love that is not fragile but alive — love that breathes, moves, and creates through you.

This is the path from survival to soul — the sacred current of life ascending through your inner river.

Bridging Root to Heart Across Cultures

Across ancient traditions, the journey from the base of the body to the center of the chest has been recognized as a sacred passage — a transformation from matter to spirit, from instinct to compassion. In yogic philosophy, this journey passes through the Root (Muladhara), the Sacral (Svadhisthana), and the Heart (Anahata) — the three chakras that form the energetic bridge between survival and love.

While the Root establishes our belonging to the earth, and the Heart opens us to divine connection, the Sacral Chakra is the living river between them — the emotional and creative current that allows life to move, feel, and flow.

Across cultures, this middle passage is portrayed through imagery of earth and water merging, body and soul uniting, and emotion serving as the bridge between survival and transcendence.

Eastern Traditions: The River of Life

In the Tantric and yogic traditions of India, the lower chakras are seen as stages of consciousness rising from dense matter to pure awareness.

- **Muladhara** represents *bhumi tattva*, the element of earth — stability, form, and structure.
- **Svadhisthana** embodies *apah tattva*, the element of water — emotion, adaptability, and sensual flow.
- **Anahata** aligns with *vayu tattva*, the element of air — movement, breath, and love.

Together, these form a natural progression: from earth to water to air — from stillness to flow to freedom. The Sacral Chakra is thus the **sacred river** connecting the ground of being with the sky of spirit. In yogic imagery, Kundalini Shakti rises through this river, learning first to move through feeling before expanding into love.

Indigenous and Shamanic Wisdom: The Heart of the Waters

In many Indigenous cosmologies, creation begins in the deep waters — the womb of the Earth Mother. These waters are both literal and symbolic: the source of fertility, emotion, and transformation.

Just as the Root connects us to the land and ancestors, the Sacral connects us to the waters of life — the emotional body, the tides of birth, and the cycles of creation. Shamans often speak of *journeying through the water realms* before reaching the upper world of spirit. The passage through the watery underworld reflects the same energetic truth: emotion must be navigated before the heart can fully open.

Taoist Philosophy: Earth, Water, and Heart Qi

In Taoist internal alchemy, energy descends from heaven and ascends from earth through the body's meridians. The lower *dantian* (energy field in the abdomen) — equivalent to the Sacral Chakra — is seen as the **cauldron of transformation**, where essence (jing) is refined into vitality (qi).

When grounded energy from the Root mixes with emotional and sexual vitality in the lower dantian, it rises naturally toward the Heart, transforming into compassion and spirit (shen). Taoists call this the "water path" — the gentle, flowing route to enlightenment — mirroring the Sacral's role as the bridge between physical grounding and emotional awakening.

Western Mysticism and Alchemy: The Marriage of Salt, Mercury, and Sulphur

In Western alchemical symbolism, spiritual transformation is achieved through the union of three elements:

- **Salt** (Earth) — the body, matter, and grounding (Root).
- **Mercury** (Water) — the emotions, adaptability, and creative flow (Sacral).
- **Sulphur** (Fire/Air) — the soul, passion, and divine love (Heart).

The alchemist's task is to balance these principles in the *alembic of the soul*, allowing the fixed (earth) and the volatile (water) to unite in harmony. This inner alchemy mirrors the chakra system: grounding, emotion, and love must be reconciled before true transformation can occur.

Psychological Perspectives: From Survival to Belonging

Modern psychology echoes the same evolutionary wisdom.

- The **Root Chakra** corresponds to the earliest developmental stage of safety and trust — the infant's need for security and physical care.
- The **Sacral Chakra** reflects the next stage — emotional development, play, and sensual exploration, where we learn to express feelings and connect with others.
- The **Heart Chakra** represents emotional maturity — the capacity for empathy, compassion, and unconditional love.

When any stage is disrupted, emotional flow becomes blocked, and love struggles to rise. Healing, therefore, involves retracing this arc — restoring safety (Root), allowing emotion (Sacral), and reopening love (Heart).

The Universal Bridge

Across all traditions, the message is the same: the passage from the Root to the Heart cannot bypass the waters of the Sacral.
You must feel before you can love.
You must flow before you can fly.
You must honor the body before you can embody the soul.

The Root grounds you in the world.
The Sacral teaches you to move with life.
The Heart reveals that love is the movement of spirit through form.

Together, they form the sacred bridge of embodiment — the living current that carries you from fear to trust, from survival to joy, from self-preservation to divine connection.

Meditation & Visualization Exercises for the Sacral Chakra

The Sacral Chakra is the temple of flow — the seat of emotion, creativity, and sensual aliveness. Meditation here is not about stilling the mind but about awakening movement, feeling, and connection. These practices invite you to soften, surrender, and trust the rhythmic pulse of life moving through you.

1. THE ORANGE LOTUS VISUALIZATION

Purpose: To awaken and balance the Sacral energy center through color and symbol.

1. Sit comfortably or lie down, placing your hands gently on your lower abdomen, just below the navel.
2. Close your eyes and breathe deeply, feeling the belly rise and fall.
3. Visualize a glowing **orange lotus** blooming in this area — six petals gently opening and closing with your breath.
4. With each inhale, see the petals absorb golden light; with each exhale, feel them radiate orange waves through your hips and lower back.
5. Whisper inwardly:
   "I flow with the rhythm of life. My emotions are sacred. My creativity is free."
6. Stay here for several minutes, allowing the warmth and color to expand until it fills your aura like the glow of a sunset reflected on calm water.

2. THE WATER FLOW MEDITATION

Purpose: To release emotional blockages and restore energetic fluidity.

1. Sit quietly and imagine yourself standing at the edge of a serene lake or river.
2. Feel the cool mist on your skin, hear the gentle ripple of water.
3. With each breath, imagine the water flowing through your body — entering through the feet, rising through the legs, swirling through the pelvis, and washing over the lower belly.
4. As it flows, it collects and carries away old emotions — fear, guilt, shame, or stagnation — returning them to the river to be purified.
5. Say silently:
   "Like water, I release. Like water, I renew."
6. When the flow feels complete, imagine the water inside you glowing with light — pure, clear, and radiant — symbolizing the emotional clarity of a balanced Sacral Chakra.

3. THE CRESCENT MOON MEDITATION

Purpose: To connect with the lunar and feminine essence of Svadhisthana.

1. Sit or recline in a dimly lit space. Visualize a **silver crescent moon** hovering just below your navel.
2. With every inhale, the moonlight brightens; with every exhale, it bathes your body in soothing radiance.
3. Feel your breath sync with the lunar rhythm — expansion and contraction, ebb and flow.
4. Allow yourself to feel your emotions as tides, gentle and natural, rising and falling within you.

5. Whisper:
    "I honor my cycles. I honor my feelings. I am one with the lunar rhythm of life."
6. Rest in the moonlight of your own being, letting calm, receptivity, and sensual peace fill your body.

4. THE PELVIC WAVE BREATH

Purpose: To awaken energy through breath and subtle movement.

1. Sit upright or lie on your back with knees bent.
2. Inhale deeply into your lower abdomen, letting the belly rise and the pelvis tilt slightly forward.
3. Exhale, drawing the navel gently toward the spine as the pelvis rocks back.
4. Continue this wave-like motion for several minutes, breathing slowly and naturally.
5. As you move, visualize orange light flowing like water through the pelvis and lower back, massaging the energy channels.
6. Repeat silently:
    "I am fluid. I am free. I am in harmony with the flow of life."
    This gentle undulation awakens creativity and emotional balance while strengthening your connection to the physical body.

5. THE SACRED RIVER VISUALIZATION

Purpose: To harmonize the Root, Sacral, and Heart chakras — connecting grounding, emotion, and love.

1. Begin by visualizing a river flowing upward through your body.
2. At the base of your spine (Root), the water emerges from the earth — solid, strong, and red.

3. As it reaches your pelvis (Sacral), it turns orange and begins to shimmer, flowing freely through the hips and belly.
4. As it rises into your chest (Heart), the water turns green, glowing with love and compassion.
5. Feel these three colors — red, orange, and green — swirling together, creating a current of grounded love and creative expression.
6. Whisper:
"From the earth I rise. Through the waters I flow. In the heart I love."
7. End the meditation by feeling your entire being as a flowing river — stable, expressive, and full of life.

6. THE BIJA MANTRA MEDITATION – VAM

Purpose: To activate the Sacral Chakra through sound vibration.

1. Sit comfortably with your spine straight.
2. Bring awareness to your lower abdomen.
3. Inhale slowly, and as you exhale, chant **VAM** (pronounced "vahm"), letting the "ah" resonate in the belly and the "m" hum softly through the pelvis.
4. Feel the vibration loosen tension, awaken pleasure, and invite warmth into the womb or hara.
5. Repeat for several minutes, then sit in silence, feeling the gentle afterglow of balance and flow.
6. Close with the affirmation:
"I honor the sacred waters within me. I am open to feeling, creating, and loving fully."

7. EMOTIONAL RELEASE AND GRATITUDE MEDITATION

Purpose: To cleanse emotional residue and restore joy.

1. Bring to mind a recent emotional experience that still lingers in your body.
2. Without judgment, breathe into it — imagine your breath wrapping it in light.
3. Exhale, letting it dissolve into the orange glow of your Sacral Chakra.
4. Now place both hands over your lower abdomen and whisper:
    "Thank you, emotion, for teaching me. I release you with love."
5. End by smiling softly into your body — a gesture of gratitude for the wisdom and flow of your inner waters.

THE ESSENCE OF PRACTICE

Sacral meditations are not about control — they are about permission.
Permission to feel.
Permission to flow.
Permission to create.
Through these practices, emotion transforms from turbulence into rhythm, pleasure becomes prayer, and the waters within you remember how to move freely again.

Crystals for the Sacral Chakra

Crystals associated with the Sacral Chakra carry the fluid, sensual, and creative vibration of water. Their energy encourages emotional healing, pleasure, and flow. These stones help dissolve shame, ignite passion, and restore balance between giving and receiving. By working with Sacral crystals, we reawaken the joy of being in our body — feeling safe to express, create, and connect.

Carnelian

- **Qualities:** Creativity, vitality, confidence.
- Known as the "artist's stone," carnelian fuels inspiration and passion. Its warm orange glow stimulates life force and helps transform lethargy into motivation. Carnelian supports the healthy expression of emotions and strengthens confidence in one's sensuality and personal power.
- **Use:** Place over the lower abdomen during meditation to awaken creative energy, wear as jewelry to enhance vitality, or keep near your workspace to inspire creative flow.

Orange Calcite

- **Qualities:** Emotional release, joy, renewal.
- Orange calcite clears stagnant emotions and uplifts the mood, acting like sunshine for the emotional body. It harmonizes the Sacral Chakra by dissolving guilt and helping one embrace pleasure without fear or judgment.
- **Use:** Hold during breathwork or energy healing to soften emotional blockages, or place near the bath to invite relaxation and joy. It's excellent for those processing emotional fatigue or creative burnout.

Moonstone

- **Qualities:** Intuition, feminine flow, emotional balance.
- Moonstone embodies the lunar qualities of reflection and renewal. It aligns with the water element and the divine feminine, supporting intuition, emotional intelligence, and cyclical rhythms. It helps one honor the natural ebb and flow of emotions.
- **Use:** Place on the lower abdomen during meditation to soothe emotional turbulence or carry it when navigating hormonal or reproductive shifts. It also supports creativity aligned with intuition and divine timing.

Sunstone

- **Qualities:** Radiance, confidence, sensual joy.
- Sunstone brings warmth and vitality to the Sacral Chakra, balancing its watery nature with the brightness of fire. It encourages self-expression, playfulness, and optimism, dispelling guilt or self-doubt.
- **Use:** Carry sunstone when you need courage to shine or to reignite enthusiasm in relationships, projects, or creative endeavors. It's especially powerful when used alongside Moonstone — uniting masculine and feminine energies in balance.

Peach Selenite

- **Qualities:** Soothing, cleansing, emotional clarity.
- Peach selenite gently clears energetic residue from past emotional wounds. Its soft, nurturing vibration promotes forgiveness, sensual healing, and peace within relationships.
- **Use:** Place at the sacral center during meditation to cleanse emotional energy or under your pillow for dream healing and emotional restoration.

HOW TO WORK WITH SACRAL CRYSTALS

- **Placement:** Lay stones on or around the lower abdomen, pelvis, or hips during energy work or meditation.
- **Water Connection:** Place crystals around your bath or in a bowl of water (check stone safety first) to charge them with the element of flow.
- **Creative Spaces:** Keep Sacral stones near your art desk, musical instruments, or journal to invite inspiration and joy.
- **Affirmation:** While holding a crystal, repeat: *"I honor my emotions. I move with life's flow. Creativity and pleasure are sacred expressions of my soul."*

Crystals for the Sacral Chakra are not only tools of beauty — they are allies for emotional liberation. Each stone carries the memory of the earth's waters, reminding us that creativity, passion, and sensuality are not indulgences but natural expressions of the divine feminine within.

CHARGING CRYSTALS WITH THE ELEMENT OF FLOW

Because the **Sacral Chakra** is governed by **water**, the act of charging your crystals with this element restores emotional fluidity, sensual vitality, and creative flow. Charging connects your stones to the frequency of movement, cleansing, and renewal — the essence of Svadhisthana itself.

1. Water Charging (Physical or Symbolic)

Water carries both memory and intention. You can use real water or simply invoke its energy.

Direct Method (for water-safe stones only):

- Place your crystal in a glass bowl of natural spring water or filtered water.
- Add a pinch of sea salt for purification (optional).
- Hold your hands above the bowl and speak an intention such as:
  "Flow through me as through these waters. Wash away what no longer serves. Renew my energy with joy."
- Leave the crystal for a few hours or overnight.

Symbolic Method (for delicate stones like selenite, calcite, or moonstone):

- Place the crystal beside a bowl of water instead of in it.
- Let it absorb the vibration of the element without physical contact.
- You can also gently mist it with charged water or use sound (singing bowl, chime) to "wash" it with frequency instead of liquid.

2. Moonlight Bathing

The moon governs the tides — and the Sacral Chakra's emotional rhythm.

- Place your crystals on a windowsill or outside under the moon, especially during a **full or waxing moon**.
- As the moonlight touches them, visualize silver-white energy flowing like water, replenishing the stones.
- Affirm: *"Under Luna's flow, my emotions and creativity are renewed."*

3. Flow Meditation Charging

For an energetic (non-physical) charge:

1. Hold your crystal in both hands over your sacral center.

2. Breathe slowly, visualizing an **orange river of light** flowing through you.
3. Let your breath mimic gentle waves — inhale rising, exhale falling.
4. Imagine this light washing through the stone, filling it with movement, joy, and sensual vitality.
5. When finished, thank the crystal and the element of water.

4. Sound as Flow

Since sound moves through air like water through a stream, it also embodies flow.

- Play ocean sounds, flowing water recordings, or use a singing bowl tuned to the note **D** (the Sacral's frequency).
- Allow the vibrations to ripple through the crystal, symbolically restoring its fluid essence.

5. Sacred Bath Ritual

For deep personal resonance:

- Place your water-safe Sacral crystals (like carnelian or orange calcite) around or near your bath.
- Add essential oils like **ylang-ylang, orange, or sandalwood**.
- As you soak, visualize your energy and the stones both recharging — the water cleansing emotions and awakening creative flow.

Charging Affirmation:

"With the power of water, I cleanse and renew.
Emotion flows freely, creation moves through me.
My crystal is alive with the rhythm of the divine current."

Essential Oils for the Sacral Chakra

The **Sacral Chakra (Svadhisthana)** is deeply responsive to warm, sweet, and exotic scents that awaken the senses, inspire creativity, and restore emotional flow. Aromas associated with **water, movement, and sensual pleasure** help dissolve stagnation, release guilt or shame, and invite joy back into the body.

Essential oils for the Sacral Chakra nurture emotional expression, intimacy, and the ability to receive life's pleasures with openness and gratitude.

Sweet Orange

- **Qualities:** Joy, flow, and emotional renewal.
- The cheerful, sunlit aroma of sweet orange uplifts the mood and restores optimism. It stimulates the creative center, dissolving self-doubt and emotional heaviness. Orange reconnects you with spontaneity and the simple pleasure of being alive.
- **Use:** Diffuse while journaling, painting, or dancing to enhance creativity; apply (diluted) to the lower abdomen to lift stagnant energy and inspire joy.

Ylang-Ylang

- **Qualities:** Sensuality, emotional release, and feminine empowerment.
- Known as the "flower of flowers," ylang-ylang balances the sacral's dual currents of passion and peace. It softens emotional tension and encourages surrender — essential qualities for allowing Shakti energy to flow freely.
- **Use:** Add to a massage blend for the hips or lower abdomen, or diffuse before meditation to awaken sensual presence and emotional openness.

Sandalwood

- **Qualities:** Sacred intimacy, creative focus, spiritual pleasure.
- Sandalwood bridges sensuality and spirituality — grounding yet transcendent. Its creamy, wood-sweet aroma harmonizes the Sacral with the Heart, transforming desire into devotion and pleasure into presence.
- **Use:** Apply diluted oil to the sacral area and heart before meditation, or add a few drops to bathwater to create a sacred ritual of self-love and embodiment.

Jasmine

- **Qualities:** Passion, confidence, and divine feminine energy.
- Jasmine's intoxicating floral aroma opens emotional gates, inspiring creativity, love, and sensuality. It is traditionally used in Tantric and devotional rituals to awaken the inner goddess — Shakti in her fullest expression.
- **Use:** Diffuse during sacred movement or creative work; apply to wrists or lower abdomen (diluted) when cultivating confidence and sensual flow.

Clary Sage

- **Qualities:** Emotional release, intuition, hormonal balance.
- Clary sage helps harmonize the body's inner tides — physical, emotional, and energetic. It soothes mood swings, enhances intuitive perception, and balances the yin–yang flow within the pelvis.
- **Use:** Inhale deeply during emotional clearing rituals or blend with orange oil in a diffuser to restore equilibrium after intense emotional release.

How to Use Sacral Chakra Oils

- **Diffusion:** Add a few drops to a diffuser to create an atmosphere of warmth, openness, and emotional flow.
- **Massage:** Blend with carrier oil and gently massage into the lower abdomen, hips, or sacral area to awaken creative and sensual energy.
- **Bath Ritual:** Add 3–5 drops to bath salts or a warm bath, imagining the water dissolving all emotional resistance and restoring pleasure to your energy field.
- **Meditation:** Place a drop on your palms, rub together, and cup over your nose while breathing deeply into the pelvis.

Affirmation to Pair with Aromatherapy

"With each breath, I awaken the river within.
Emotion flows freely, creativity moves through me,
and I embrace the joy of being alive."

Energetic Insight

Essential oils for the Sacral Chakra are not just fragrances — they are **vibrations of pleasure and flow.** Each scent reminds the body that it is safe to feel, to express, and to create. Through the sense of smell, the most primal and emotional of our senses, these oils invite us to reclaim the sacredness of sensation and the beauty of embodiment.

BLENDING FOR FLOW: ESSENTIAL OIL COMBINATIONS FOR THE SACRAL CHAKRA

Blending essential oils for the Sacral Chakra is an act of artistry — the merging of scent, sensation, and emotion. Each blend becomes a form of vibrational alchemy, awakening movement where there was stagnation and joy where there was numbness. Because the Sacral is governed by water, blends should feel **fluid, harmonizing, and emotionally evocative**, helping energy move with grace rather than force.

When creating your blend, focus on **intention** — your reason for blending is the soul of the formula. Combine up to three oils in a carrier base such as jojoba, coconut, or apricot kernel oil. Shake gently and infuse your blend with awareness before using.

1. Flow & Creativity

Purpose: To awaken inspiration and emotional expression.
Blend:

- 2 drops Sweet Orange
- 2 drops Clary Sage
- 1 drop Sandalwood
  Use: Diffuse while journaling, painting, or brainstorming. You can also apply a drop (diluted) to your wrists and breathe deeply before creative work.
  Affirmation: "My creativity flows like a river — effortless, radiant, and alive."

2. Sensual Awakening

Purpose: To reconnect with sensual presence and embodied pleasure.
Blend:

- 2 drops Ylang-Ylang
- 1 drop Jasmine
- 1 drop Patchouli
  Use: Add to warm bathwater or use as a body anointing oil before meditation or movement. Let your body lead, without judgment.
  Affirmation: "I honor the sacred within my senses. Pleasure is divine."

3. Emotional Release

Purpose: To dissolve emotional blocks and restore flow.
Blend:

- 2 drops Clary Sage
- 2 drops Bergamot
- 1 drop Vetiver
  Use: Massage into the lower abdomen while breathing deeply; visualize stagnant emotions flowing out like gentle waves returning to the sea.
  Affirmation: "I release what no longer serves me. My emotions move freely and heal me."

4. Inner Harmony

Purpose: To balance the feminine and masculine energies within.
Blend:

- 1 drop Sandalwood
- 2 drops Orange
- 1 drop Lavender
  Use: Diffuse during meditation or apply over the sacral area. The warm wood of sandalwood grounds, while orange uplifts and lavender soothes.
  Affirmation: "Within me, energy and awareness dance in perfect rhythm."

5. Sacred Waters Ritual Blend

Purpose: To honor Shakti — the creative, flowing life force within.
Blend:

- 1 drop Jasmine
- 1 drop Ylang-Ylang
- 1 drop Rose (or Geranium as substitute)
  Use: Add to a ritual bath or anoint candles before meditation. As the aroma fills the air, imagine your energy body glowing with soft orange light — fluid, radiant, and alive.
  Affirmation: "I am the river of life. My energy flows with grace and purpose."

Charging Your Blends with the Element of Flow

Because the Sacral Chakra is ruled by **water**, charge your oil blends with this element to amplify their vibration:

1. **Moonlight Charging:** Place your blend in a glass container under the moon (especially the full or waxing moon) overnight to absorb lunar energy.
2. **Water Bowl Ritual:** Float your blend bottle in a bowl of water while meditating on emotional release and flow.
3. **Sound Infusion:** Gently chant the bija mantra **"VAM"** over your blend seven times to attune it to the frequency of Svadhisthana.

CRYSTAL + AROMA ACTIVATION FOR EMOTIONAL FLOW

The Sacral Chakra is awakened not by effort, but by *sensation*. It opens when emotion, scent, touch, and energy move in harmony — when body and spirit remember that flow is natural.

This ritual unites two powerful allies — **crystals** and **essential oils** — to restore rhythm, pleasure, and creativity to your energetic waters.

Preparation

Set aside 10–15 minutes in a quiet, softly lit space.
Wear loose clothing, and if possible, sit or recline near water — a bath, bowl, or even a gentle fountain.
Have these items ready:

- **One Sacral Crystal:** Carnelian, orange calcite, moonstone, or peach aventurine.
- **Your Flow Blend:** Any essential oil blend created in the previous section (or simply Sweet Orange and Ylang-Ylang diluted in a carrier oil).
- **A small candle** or soft instrumental music (optional).

1. Centering Breath

Begin with three deep breaths.
Inhale through the nose, allowing your abdomen to expand.
Exhale through the mouth, releasing any tension in the hips, belly, or lower back.
Feel your breath move like gentle waves — rising, falling, flowing.

Whisper:
"I soften. I allow. I flow."

2. Anointing the Energy Center

Warm a few drops of your oil blend between your palms.
Bring your hands over your **lower abdomen**, just below the navel — the home of Svadhisthana.
As you inhale, feel the aroma rise through your senses.

As you exhale, imagine orange light swirling beneath your palms, like sunlight rippling on water.

If you wish, lightly anoint the following points:

- **Lower abdomen** (emotional center)
- **Inner wrists** (expression and pulse of flow)
- **Heart center** (to connect emotion with love)

Affirm softly:
"I honor my emotions. I move with life's rhythm."

3. Crystal Infusion

Hold your chosen crystal in your right hand (the giving hand). Close your eyes and visualize drawing energy up from the earth — warm, orange-gold light flowing into the crystal.
Now move the crystal over your sacral area in slow, circular motions.
With each circle, imagine the light growing brighter, warmer, more fluid.

Repeat the mantra:
"VAM"
Let the vibration ripple through your pelvis — low, soft, resonant.

4. The Flow Meditation

Place the crystal gently over your lower abdomen (or in front of you if lying down).
Visualize a pool of water inside your body — calm, luminous, and alive.
Each breath sends ripples through it.
With every exhale, release old emotions, guilt, or fear.
With every inhale, invite in joy, sensuality, and creativity.

See this water begin to shimmer and dance — alive with orange and silver light.
Let your whole being sway gently, as though moved by an inner tide.

5. Integration

When you feel complete, bring one hand to your **heart** and one to your **sacral center**.
Feel the bridge between love and emotion — between Anahata and Svadhisthana — glowing in unity.
Whisper to yourself:

"My heart blesses my emotions. My emotions serve my heart. I am in harmony."

Take a few deep breaths and slowly open your eyes.
You may wish to write, draw, or dance to express what has moved within you.

Aftercare

- **Cleanse** your crystal under cool running water or moonlight.
- **Store** your oil blend in a sacred space.
- **Repeat** this ritual weekly or during the waxing moon to encourage creativity and emotional vitality.

WATER RITUAL FOR EMOTIONAL RENEWAL
A Sacral Chakra Bath & Moon Water Ceremony

Water is the sacred element of Svadhisthana — the mirror of emotion, creativity, and flow.
When we immerse ourselves in water with intention, we return to the womb of creation, where emotion becomes movement and every wave carries the potential for rebirth.

This ritual can be performed in a **bath**, **natural body of water**, or even as a **bowl ceremony** if immersion isn't possible.
Its purpose is to **cleanse emotional residue, reignite creative flow**, and **reconnect to the sensual wisdom of the body.**

Preparation: Setting the Energy of Flow

Choose a time when you will not be disturbed.
For deeper resonance, perform this ritual during a **waxing or full moon**, when water energy is most receptive.

Gather:

- A bowl or tub of **warm water**
- 1–2 drops of **Ylang-Ylang** or **Sweet Orange** essential oil
- A handful of **Epsom or Himalayan salt** (for release and purification)
- One **Sacral crystal** (Carnelian, Moonstone, or Orange Calcite)
- Optional: **Floating candle, orange or coral cloth, soft music**

Take a moment to light your candle and whisper:
"I enter the waters of renewal. I return to flow."

Step 1: Blessing the Waters

Hold your hands over the water and breathe deeply.
Imagine drawing in orange light through your crown, then exhaling it through your hands into the bowl or bath.
Visualize the water glowing with this light — alive, swirling, conscious.

Say aloud or in your heart:
"Waters of life, I honor your wisdom.
Cleanse me of what no longer serves.
Awaken my joy, creativity, and flow."

Drop in your crystal and let it rest at the bottom or in your palm
if you are bathing.

Step 2: Immersion and Release

Enter the water slowly, allowing your body to relax fully.
Close your eyes.
Feel the temperature, the texture, the soft buoyancy supporting
you.
With each breath, surrender more deeply to the water's
embrace.

As you exhale, imagine emotional heaviness — guilt, shame, or
sorrow — flowing out through your pores and dissolving into
the water.
With each inhale, feel your body filling with orange-gold light
— vibrant, sensual, creative.

Whisper:
"I release control. I trust the current of life."

Step 3: Stirring the Waters

If you are in a bath, gently swirl the water with your hands.
If using a bowl, use your fingertips to create small circles,
watching the ripples spread outward.
This movement symbolizes the dance of emotion — how every
feeling creates a wave, yet always returns to stillness.

As the water moves, chant softly:
VAM... VAM... VAM...
Let the vibration ripple through your body and into the water.

Imagine it awakening your inner tide — the rhythm of your soul.

Step 4: Reclaiming Joy and Sensual Presence

When you feel clear and light, bring both hands to your **lower abdomen**.
Visualize a lotus opening in a pool of radiant orange light.
See it pulsing with life, creativity, and pleasure.

Say to yourself:
**"I am free to feel. I am free to create.
My emotions are sacred. My body is divine."**

Breathe into that truth until your whole being feels warm and alive.

Step 5: Completion and Offering

When ready, drain or pour out the water mindfully.
If in a bath, visualize all heaviness flowing away into the earth for transformation.
If using a bowl, pour the water outdoors or into the soil as an offering, saying:
"As I am cleansed, may the earth be blessed."

Dry your body gently, keeping awareness in your lower belly.
If possible, spend a few minutes journaling or drawing — capturing whatever emotions or visions surfaced during the ritual.

Optional: Charging Moon Water for Ongoing Flow

1. Fill a glass jar with clean water.
2. Place your **sacral crystal** beside or inside it (ensure the crystal is safe for water).
3. Set it beneath the **moonlight overnight** with the intention of emotional renewal and creativity.
4. In the morning, use the water to anoint your wrists, belly, or add a few drops to your bath.

Each time, whisper:
"I move with life. I flow with grace."

The Hidden Wisdom

In Tantra, water is not just an element — it is consciousness in motion.
By honoring it through ritual, you awaken the same consciousness within yourself.
Emotion no longer overwhelms you; it becomes your teacher.
Pleasure no longer distracts; it becomes your prayer.
Through water, you remember that *to feel is to live* — and to live is to flow.

Somatic Practices for the Sacral Chakra

Reconnecting to the Body Through Movement and Sensation

While meditation stills the mind, **somatic practices** awaken the body.
The Sacral Chakra — *Svadhisthana*, the seat of emotion, creativity, and sensual flow — thrives on movement. Unlike the Root, which grounds, the Sacral invites motion, rhythm, and expression. Healing this chakra means learning to feel *safe within movement*, to trust the body's sensations, and to let emotion become energy in motion.

When trauma, guilt, or suppression have numbed the body, somatic awareness restores vitality. It teaches us to listen again — to the hips, the belly, the breath, and the tides of emotion that move through them.

Below are practices designed to help the waters of Svadhisthana flow freely while keeping awareness anchored in the body.

1. Pelvic Breath: Awakening the Inner Tide

The pelvic breath connects breath to the body's natural rhythm, stimulating circulation and emotional release in the lower abdomen.

Practice:

1. Sit or lie comfortably with one hand on your lower belly and one on your chest.
2. Inhale deeply through the nose, expanding the belly before the chest.
3. Exhale slowly through the mouth, softening the hips and pelvic floor.
4. Feel the gentle wave of breath rising and falling between your navel and pubic bone.
5. Continue for 3–5 minutes, allowing the motion to become fluid and effortless.

Mantra:
"With every breath, I awaken flow within me."

2. Hip Circles: Releasing Stored Emotion

The hips are the body's emotional vault. Gentle circular movements loosen energetic blockages and restore sensual confidence.

Practice:

1. Stand with feet shoulder-width apart, knees slightly bent.
2. Place hands on hips and begin to rotate them in wide, slow circles.
3. Move clockwise for a few breaths, then counterclockwise.
4. Keep the movement smooth and rhythmic — like drawing infinity signs with your pelvis.
5. Allow the breath to follow the motion, releasing any tightness or resistance.

As the hips move, emotions may rise — warmth, tenderness, or even tears. Let them flow. This is energy becoming free again.

3. Wave Movement: Embodying Flow

This movement practice imitates the natural undulation of water — the essence of the Sacral Chakra.

Practice:

1. Stand tall with feet rooted, knees soft.
2. Begin to sway gently from side to side, letting your spine move like a wave.
3. Allow the shoulders, ribs, and hips to follow — fluid, unforced, continuous.
4. Feel how the wave begins in the pelvis and rises through the spine.
5. Continue for several minutes, breathing naturally, eyes closed if comfortable.

Intention:
To reconnect your awareness to rhythm, breath, and the sensual intelligence of the body.

4. Belly Release: Softening the Core

Modern culture teaches us to hold in the belly — to appear flat, strong, or "controlled."
Yet emotional healing requires softness. The belly houses both the Sacral and Solar Plexus chakras, and relaxing it allows energy to move again.

Practice:

1. Lie on your back with knees bent.
2. Place one hand on your lower belly.
3. Inhale deeply, letting your abdomen rise freely.
4. As you exhale, gently sigh or hum, releasing tension.
5. Whisper to yourself:
   "It is safe to soften. My feelings can move."

This simple act — of allowing the belly to expand and release — signals safety to the nervous system and reawakens embodied trust.

5. Somatic Expression: Dance of Emotion

The Sacral Chakra heals through **expression**. When emotion is repressed, energy stagnates. When expressed consciously — through movement, sound, or art — it transforms into freedom.

Practice:

1. Play instrumental music that feels emotional but fluid — such as drums, cello, or ambient soundscapes.
2. Close your eyes and let your body respond. Move slowly, intuitively.
3. Let every gesture reflect what you feel: expansion, grief, joy, desire, surrender.

4. If words arise, speak or hum them softly.
5. When the movement ends, stand still and place your hands on your heart and belly. Feel the afterglow of release.

Reflection Prompt:
What emotion did my body want to express today?

6. Womb or Hara Meditation

Regardless of gender, the energetic womb (for women) or hara (for men) is the creative center of being — the point of stillness within motion.

Practice:

1. Sit with hands cupped over the lower belly.
2. Breathe gently into this space, imagining a soft, glowing orange light expanding with each inhale.
3. On the exhale, feel that light pulsing outward in waves — radiating calm pleasure through your whole body.
4. Remain in this awareness for several minutes.

Mantra:
"My center is fluid, creative, and alive."

The Somatic Wisdom of the Sacral

These practices restore the dialogue between body and soul. They remind us that emotion is not meant to be analyzed — it is meant to be felt, moved, and released.
As you continue working with Svadhisthana, you may find that creativity returns effortlessly, relationships deepen, and your natural sensuality awakens — not as indulgence, but as reverence for life's rhythm.

When the body flows, the soul breathes.
When the soul breathes, healing begins.

Yoga and Breathwork for the Sacral Chakra

Awakening Flow, Sensuality, and Emotional Freedom

The Sacral Chakra (*Svadhisthana*) governs movement, pleasure, and emotional expression — all of which thrive through fluidity. Yoga and breathwork are among the most powerful tools for restoring balance here because they bridge body, breath, and energy.

While Root Chakra yoga emphasizes stillness and grounding, **Sacral Chakra practices emphasize movement, rhythm, and flow.** These sequences and breathing techniques awaken the hips, lower abdomen, and pelvis — the physical home of Svadhisthana — and help release emotional stagnation stored within the body's waters.

The Element of Water in Yoga

Svadhisthana corresponds to **water**, representing adaptability, feeling, and surrender.
The goal of Sacral Yoga is not rigidity or control, but *fluid embodiment.*
When practiced consciously, each pose becomes a wave — inhaling to expand, exhaling to release — awakening the sensual and creative currents within.

Intention for Practice:
"I move like water — fluid, free, and alive."

YOGA POSES FOR THE SACRAL CHAKRA

Each of the following postures supports flexibility, flow, and openness in the hips, pelvis, and lower spine — regions often associated with stored emotion or creative stagnation.

1. Bound Angle Pose (Baddha Konasana) – Opening the Inner Waters

Sit with the soles of the feet together and knees dropping out to the sides.
Hold the feet with both hands and allow the spine to lengthen upward.
Breathe gently into the hips, letting the knees lower with gravity.
Focus: Softening resistance and inviting emotional release.
Affirmation: "It is safe to open and feel."

2. Goddess Pose (Utkata Konasana) – Embodying Sensual Power

Stand with feet wide apart, toes turned out, knees bent deeply.
Press palms together at the heart or extend arms wide.
Sway the hips gently side to side as you breathe deeply.
Focus: Strength within fluidity — grounded yet free.
Affirmation: "I embrace my power and sensual strength."

3. Pigeon Pose (Eka Pada Rajakapotasana) – Releasing Stored Emotion

From the tabletop, bring one knee forward and extend the other leg back.
Fold forward over the front leg, resting the forehead on hands or a block.
Breathe into the hips, exhaling tension or suppressed feelings.
Focus: Releasing emotional weight held in the pelvis.
Affirmation: "I release the past and flow freely with life."

4. Seated Forward Fold (Paschimottanasana) – Flowing Inward

Sit tall with legs extended, hinge forward from the hips, and reach for your feet or shins.
Allow the spine to lengthen on each inhale and soften on each exhale.
Focus: Surrender and emotional introspection.
Affirmation: "I trust the rhythm of my life."

5. Cat–Cow (Marjaryasana–Bitilasana) – The Dance of the Spine

On hands and knees, alternate arching and rounding the spine.
Let the movement become sensual — led by the pelvis, not the head.
Coordinate each motion with breath: inhale to open, exhale to contract.
Focus: Fluid movement, releasing rigidity, awakening pleasure in motion.
Affirmation: "I move with grace and ease."

6. Reclined Butterfly (Supta Baddha Konasana) – Receiving Flow

Lie on your back with the soles of the feet together, knees open.
Rest your hands on the belly and heart.
Breathe deeply, allowing energy to circulate between these centers.
Focus: Integration — the flow of love between heart and womb/hara.
Affirmation: "I receive pleasure and life with an open heart."

Breathwork for the Sacral Chakra

Breath is the bridge between emotion and energy. In the Sacral Chakra, **breath mirrors water** — flowing, undulating, continuous. Breathwork helps restore rhythm to emotions, regulate sensitivity, and release energetic blockages held in the pelvic region.

1. Wave Breath

This breathing pattern mimics the movement of the ocean — the natural rhythm of expansion and release.

Practice:

1. Sit or lie comfortably.
2. Inhale deeply into the lower belly, letting it rise like a wave.
3. Continue inhaling into the ribs and chest.
4. Exhale smoothly from chest to belly, letting the "wave" return to shore.
5. Continue for several minutes, visualizing orange light flowing through your hips and abdomen.

Effect: Restores flow, emotional balance, and sensual vitality.
Mantra: "I breathe in pleasure. I exhale resistance."

2. Cooling Breath (Shitali Pranayama)

When the Sacral is overactive — emotions heightened or desires overwhelming — this breath cools and soothes the waters.

Practice:

1. Roll the tongue into a tube (or press lips into an 'O' if unable).
2. Inhale slowly through the mouth, feeling cool air flow down to the pelvis.
3. Exhale through the nose with awareness in the lower belly.
4. Continue for 5–10 rounds.

Effect: Calms overstimulation, balances fire within water.
Mantra: "I am calm, centered, and serene."

3. Pelvic Pulse Breath

This practice awakens the Sacral's rhythmic intelligence — the pulse of life itself.

Practice:

1. Sit or stand with hands on the lower belly.
2. As you inhale, gently contract the pelvic floor (mula bandha).
3. As you exhale, release and soften completely.
4. Continue for 2–3 minutes, synchronizing breath with subtle movement.

Effect: Strengthens the energetic foundation, enhances creative energy flow, and balances sensual vitality.

4. Nadi Shodhana (Alternate Nostril Breathing)

To balance left–right polarity (feminine/masculine energy) within the Sacral.

Practice:

1. Use the right thumb to close the right nostril. Inhale through the left.
2. Close the left nostril with the ring finger. Exhale through the right.
3. Inhale through the right, close, and exhale through the left.
4. Continue for several minutes, keeping breath smooth and gentle.

Effect: Harmonizes emotional and creative energies, balances receptivity and action.

Integrating the Practice

After your yoga and breathwork session, sit quietly with your hands on your lower belly.
Feel the gentle hum of energy moving within.
Notice any emotional shifts — a sense of lightness, warmth, or fluid ease.

Reflection:
The Sacral Chakra teaches that movement is healing.
Through yoga and breathwork, you remember that emotion and creativity are not obstacles to spirituality — they are its flowing essence.

Closing Affirmation:
"I move with life. I breathe with ease. I create with joy."

Healing Through Water Rituals and Moon Cycles

Honoring the Element of Flow and the Feminine Rhythms of Life

The Sacral Chakra (*Svadhisthana*) is ruled by the **element of water** and the **cyclical wisdom of the moon**.
Both are symbols of rhythm, emotion, and the power of change.
Just as the tides are shaped by the moon's pull, our emotions, creativity, and sensuality rise and fall in natural waves.
To heal and balance the Sacral Chakra is to honor these cycles — to surrender to flow rather than resist it.

Water as a Sacred Healer

Water holds memory.
It absorbs vibration, emotion, and intention.
Cultures throughout history — from Hindu ritual baths in the Ganges to Celtic holy wells and Japanese purification ceremonies — have understood water as a living consciousness capable of renewal.

When working with the Sacral Chakra, **water becomes your teacher.**
It teaches fluidity, adaptability, and release.
Where earth grounds, water transforms. It does not fight the rock in its path — it shapes it through time.

Intention for Practice:
"Like water, I flow freely and return to calm."

Water Ritual for Emotional Release

This ritual helps clear stagnant energy, emotional residue, and creative blockages from the Sacral Chakra.

You'll Need:

- A warm bath (or bowl of water if bathing isn't possible)
- 3 drops of essential oils such as **ylang ylang, orange, or clary sage**
- A handful of **Epsom or Himalayan salt**
- A **candle** (orange or white) to represent the inner flame of creation

Steps:

1. **Prepare the Water:**
   Light the candle and whisper your intention:
   "As this water receives me, may it cleanse all that I no longer need."
   Add the salt and oils, stirring clockwise to charge the water with flow.
2. **Enter or Touch the Water:**
   If bathing, immerse slowly, feeling warmth surround your hips and belly.
   If using a bowl, dip your hands and gently anoint your lower abdomen.
3. **Breathe and Release:**
   Inhale deeply through the nose, exhale through the mouth with sound — sighs, hums, or tones that express emotion.
   Let tears, laughter, or silence come naturally.
4. **Seal the Ritual:**
   Whisper: *"I am fluid. I am free. I flow with life."*
   When finished, pour the water onto the earth or down the drain, imagining it carrying away all emotional residue.

Purpose:
This simple act of bathing becomes a sacrament — a remembrance that cleansing is not just physical but energetic.

Water teaches that every emotion is temporary, every wave returns to stillness.

Moon Cycles and the Sacral Rhythm

The Sacral Chakra is deeply influenced by **the moon**, symbol of the divine feminine and the cyclical nature of all life.
Its Sanskrit name, *Svadhisthana*, means "one's own abode," reflecting the sacred rhythm of being in tune with one's inner tides.

Each lunar phase mirrors a different aspect of the Sacral's wisdom:

Moon Phase	Energy Focus	Sacral Reflection
New Moon	Rest, introspection, setting new creative intentions	"I listen within the still waters."
Waxing Moon	Growth, exploration, experimentation	"My creativity expands and takes form."
Full Moon	Expression, sensual fullness, emotional illumination	"I celebrate my wholeness and desire."
Waning Moon	Release, surrender, emotional cleansing	"I let go and flow back to peace."

Working consciously with these phases aligns your emotional and creative cycles with nature's rhythm.
It reminds you that you are not meant to be in constant motion — rest and release are as sacred as creation.

Lunar Water Activation

This gentle monthly ritual charges water with lunar energy to harmonize the Sacral Chakra.

You'll Need:

- A glass bowl or jar of pure water
- A moonlit night (especially New or Full Moon)
- Optional: orange carnelian or moonstone

Steps:

1. Place the water in moonlight overnight.
2. Speak or write an affirmation, such as:
   "I honor the flow of my emotions and the rhythm of the moon within me."
3. In the morning, use this water to anoint your wrists, heart, and lower abdomen — or sip a few drops mindfully, feeling the lunar vibration enter your system.

Purpose:
Lunar water reconnects you with natural cycles — reminding you that creativity and emotion wax and wane, just as the moon does.

Flow Ritual: Movement and Emotion

When emotions feel stuck, movement becomes medicine. This short ritual blends water and motion to free the Sacral currents.

Steps:

1. Play soft, flowing music with a steady rhythm.
2. Stand with feet wide, knees slightly bent.
3. Begin to sway your hips gently — side to side, front to back, then in slow circles.
4. Let your arms follow naturally, as if you are waves rising and falling.
5. Imagine orange light swirling through your lower belly, glowing brighter with each breath.

Affirmation:
"My emotions move through me like water. I do not resist — I flow."

Purpose:
This ritual reawakens sensuality and spontaneity, releasing emotional tension through embodied rhythm.
When the body flows, the soul follows.

The Lesson of Water and Moon

Both water and moon remind us that change is not loss — it is life's natural motion.
The tides ebb and return, emotions rise and fall, creativity waxes and wanes.

The Sacral Chakra teaches that there is beauty in rhythm — in the dance between fullness and emptiness, giving and receiving, joy and release.
To live by the flow is to trust that what leaves will return, transformed.

Closing Reflection:
"As the moon waxes and wanes, so too do I.
I am a vessel of flow, a tide of emotion, a river of creation.
In honoring my cycles, I honor life itself."

Affirmations, Mudras, and Daily Balancing Practices for the Sacral Chakra

Awakening Flow, Creativity, and Emotional Harmony

The Sacral Chakra is the wellspring of your emotional intelligence, sensuality, and creative life force.
To balance it is to remember how to flow with life — to move with grace rather than resistance, to feel deeply without drowning, and to create from joy instead of need.
Daily rituals, affirmations, and hand mudras act as simple yet potent tools to keep this energy center open, fluid, and aligned.

AFFIRMATIONS FOR EMOTIONAL FLOW AND CREATIVE RENEWAL

Words carry vibration — when spoken with intention, they reprogram the body's energetic blueprint.
These affirmations strengthen emotional trust, awaken pleasure, and restore connection to your inner rhythm.
Speak them aloud, slowly, while resting a hand on your lower abdomen and breathing deeply.

Morning Activation Affirmations

- "I allow my emotions to flow freely and without judgment."
- "My creativity moves through me effortlessly."
- "Pleasure is sacred, and I honor it with gratitude."
- "I trust the flow of life and my place within it."
- "I am safe to feel, to express, and to create."

Evening Integration Affirmations

- "I release what I no longer need and return to stillness."
- "My emotions guide me with wisdom and clarity."

- "I am nourished by the waters of my being."
- "Each day, I create beauty from within."
- "I am in harmony with the tides of my soul."

Mantra for Meditation
VAM — (pronounced "vahm")
Chant this bija sound softly during meditation to awaken the
Sacral's element of water.
Feel the vibration in your pelvis and lower abdomen, rippling
like gentle waves through your energy field.

MUDRAS FOR BALANCING THE SACRAL CHAKRA

In yogic tradition, *mudras* (hand gestures) are sacred seals that
direct the body's energy flow.
When paired with breath and awareness, they awaken and
balance the subtle body.
The following mudras specifically harmonize the fluid element
of Svadhisthana.

1. Shakti Mudra — The Gesture of Creative Power

This mudra honors Shakti, the divine feminine energy of
creation and flow.
It calms the nervous system and deepens emotional awareness.

How to Practice:

1. Sit comfortably with your spine straight.
2. Touch the tips of your ring fingers and little fingers
   together.
3. Fold your middle and index fingers inward toward your
   palms, resting your thumbs lightly on them.
4. Hold near the lower abdomen and breathe deeply for 5–
   10 minutes.

Affirmation:
"I honor the sacred feminine within. My creativity flows with ease."

2. Varuna Mudra — The Seal of Water Balance

Named after Varuna, the Vedic deity of cosmic waters, this mudra restores emotional equilibrium and supports hydration and vitality.

How to Practice:

1. Touch the tip of your little finger to the tip of your thumb on each hand.
2. Keep the other fingers extended and relaxed.
3. Rest your hands on your knees, palms upward.
4. Practice for 10–15 minutes, breathing slowly.

Affirmation:
"My emotions are fluid, balanced, and clear like water."

3. Yoni Mudra — The Gesture of the Sacred Womb

Symbolizing the creative matrix of life, this mudra grounds you in sensual awareness and inner calm.
It harmonizes reproductive energy and supports the healing of emotional blockages.

How to Practice:

1. Bring your hands together in front of your pelvis.
2. Touch the tips of your thumbs and index fingers together to form a downward-pointing triangle.
3. Relax your shoulders and breathe into the space within your hands.
4. Feel warmth and expansion in your lower belly.

Affirmation:
"Within me lies the power to create, to feel, and to be reborn."

DAILY BALANCING PRACTICES

The Sacral Chakra thrives on rhythm — daily actions that echo the cycles of breath, water, and moonlight.
Integrating these gentle practices can sustain harmony and awaken joy.

1. The Flow Ritual (Morning or Evening)

Begin or end each day with five minutes of mindful movement.
Let your hips sway, your spine ripple, and your breath lead the dance.
Allow yourself to feel — not perform — each motion.
This awakens Shakti and invites flow into every aspect of life.

2. Creative Pulse Practice

Spend a few minutes each day creating — doodling, singing, journaling, cooking, or arranging flowers.
Don't judge the result; feel the process.
This honors Svadhisthana's truth: *creativity is not something you do — it is what you are.*

3. Water Connection

Drink water slowly and consciously, blessing each sip.
Take baths, swim, or spend time near lakes, rivers, or the sea.
As you connect with water, whisper:
"As water flows, so do I. As water softens, so does my heart."

4. Sensual Mindfulness

Throughout the day, bring attention to your senses.
Notice texture, color, scent, and sound.

Pleasure lives in the present — and by honoring your senses, you return to it.

5. Journaling Prompts for Emotional Clarity

- What emotion am I resisting today, and what might it want to teach me?
- Where in my life am I holding back flow?
- What creative expression feels most alive in me right now?
- What would it look like to experience pleasure without guilt or hesitation?

Closing Reflection

When the Sacral Chakra is balanced, life becomes art.
Emotion moves without fear, pleasure becomes prayer, and creation becomes communion with the divine.
Every feeling, movement, and breath becomes part of your sacred dance with life.

Affirmation to End Practice:
"I honor my emotions as sacred messengers.
I celebrate my sensual, creative nature.
I flow with the rhythm of life —
and in my flow, I find freedom."

Food Therapy for the Sacral Chakra

Nourishing Flow, Pleasure, and Emotional Balance

The Sacral Chakra thrives on **hydration, sweetness, and flow** — both literal and emotional. Because this chakra is governed by the element of **water**, foods that are juicy, colorful, and vibrant help restore its balance. Eating for Svadhisthana is not only about nutrition but also about pleasure: the sensory experience of taste, texture, scent, and satisfaction.

When balanced, you eat with awareness and joy, savoring each bite as an act of gratitude and connection. When blocked, eating may become rushed, numb, or emotionally charged — too much control or too much indulgence. The key is to **return eating to ritual**, allowing nourishment to become a sensual meditation.

Energetic Principles

- **Element:** Water
- **Sense:** Taste
- **Color:** Orange
- **Location:** Lower abdomen, pelvis, reproductive organs
- **Themes:** Pleasure, flow, creativity, sensuality, emotional release

FOODS THAT HEAL AND BALANCE THE SACRAL CHAKRA

Orange-Colored Fruits and Vegetables

The natural orange hue of foods corresponds to the vibration of the Sacral Chakra.
These foods are rich in **beta-carotene**, which supports reproductive health, skin vitality, and emotional stability.

- Carrots, sweet potatoes, yams
- Oranges, mandarins, mangoes, papayas, peaches, apricots
- Butternut squash, pumpkin

How to Use:
Steam or roast for warmth and softness — the Sacral loves *comfort textures.*
Blend into soups or smoothies for hydration and color therapy.

Hydrating and Flow-Inducing Foods

Since Svadhisthana is the seat of water energy, hydration is essential.
Choose foods that replenish fluids and encourage detoxification through gentle flow.

- Coconut water
- Cucumber, watermelon, zucchini
- Celery, lettuce, leafy greens
- Herbal teas (especially chamomile, hibiscus, or rooibos)

Ritual Practice:
Drink a glass of water with mindfulness each morning.
Whisper an intention: *"As water flows through me, emotions move freely."*

Sweet and Satisfying Nourishment

Natural sweetness balances the emotional body, offering comfort without excess.
It restores sensual pleasure to eating, reminding us that joy is part of nourishment.

- Honey, dates, figs, apricots
- Cinnamon, vanilla, nutmeg (aromatic warming spices)
- Cooked grains like basmati rice, oats, quinoa with a touch of sweetness

Avoid:
Overprocessed sugars, which create emotional highs and crashes that unbalance the Sacral's rhythm.

Healthy Fats for Hormonal Harmony

The Sacral Chakra governs the reproductive organs and hormonal flow.

Healthy fats nourish this system and stabilize mood, enhancing both sensual and emotional wellbeing.

- Avocados, coconuts
- Nuts and seeds (especially almonds, flax, pumpkin, sunflower)
- Olive oil, sesame oil, hemp oil

Tip:
Massage warm sesame or coconut oil into the lower abdomen to nourish the Sacral both inside and out.

Warming and Circulatory Spices

Mildly warming foods encourage circulation, awakening sensual energy and metabolism.

- Ginger, cardamom, cinnamon, turmeric, coriander

These spices also support digestion — a key function in emotional processing.
When digestion flows, so does emotion.

FOODS TO BALANCE EXCESS SACRAL ENERGY

When the Sacral Chakra is overactive, emotions and desires can overflow.
Grounding and neutral foods help restore equilibrium.

- Brown rice, lentils, root vegetables (carrots, beets)
- Cooling teas like peppermint or spearmint
- Moderate use of dairy or coconut milk to soothe heat

HEALING RITUAL: THE SENSUAL EATING PRACTICE

1. Choose one meal per day to eat *without distraction.*
2. Before eating, look at your food — notice its color, shape, scent.
3. Inhale deeply, offering gratitude to the water, sun, and soil that created it.
4. Take slow bites, savoring texture and flavor.
5. With each swallow, imagine your Sacral Chakra glowing brighter — warm, orange, fluid.

This ritual restores the pleasure and presence that modern eating often loses.

AFFIRMATION FOR FOOD AS FLOW

"Every sip, every bite is an offering to life.
I honor the waters within me that nourish creation, emotion, and joy."

Herbal & Tea Therapy for the Sacral Chakra

Supporting Emotional Flow, Hormonal Harmony, and Creative Energy

Herbs for the Sacral Chakra work like gentle rivers — they move, soothe, and nourish.
Because *Svadhisthana* governs the reproductive organs, emotions, and fluids of the body, its balance depends on herbs that **support circulation, ease emotional tension, and harmonize hormones.**

When the Sacral is blocked, herbs can help emotions flow again; when it's overstimulated, they bring calm.

They invite balance between passion and peace — restoring pleasure as a sacred experience, not a distraction.

ENERGETIC PRINCIPLES

- **Element:** Water
- **Function:** Flow, emotion, sensuality, creativity, fertility
- **Primary Organs:** Reproductive system, kidneys, bladder, lymphatic system
- **Keywords:** Flow, nourish, harmonize, release

HERBS TO AWAKEN AND BALANCE THE SACRAL CHAKRA
Damiana (Turnera diffusa)

- **Energetic Action:** Aphrodisiac, uplifting, harmonizing.
- **Benefits:** Stimulates sensuality and creativity; uplifts mood and relieves emotional tension.
- **Use:** Brew as a tea alone or in blends; excellent before journaling, dancing, or romantic connection.
- **Spiritual Quality:** Encourages openness and receptivity — awakening joy without excess.

Orange Peel

- **Energetic Action:** Brightening, moving, and emotionally clearing.
- **Benefits:** Supports digestion (emotional and physical), enhances joy, and helps release stored resentment.
- **Use:** Add dried orange peel to teas for lightness and warmth.
- **Spiritual Quality:** Restores zest for life — helps you "taste" joy again.

Hibiscus

- **Energetic Action:** Cooling, cleansing, heart-opening.
- **Benefits:** Supports circulation, balances temperature and hormones, and uplifts mood.
- **Use:** Steep as a ruby-red tea to refresh body and spirit.
- **Spiritual Quality:** Symbol of feminine grace and flow — it teaches beauty through surrender.

Shatavari (Asparagus racemosus)

- **Energetic Action:** Restorative, nourishing, deeply feminine.
- **Benefits:** Tonic for hormonal balance, fertility, and reproductive vitality. Especially supportive for women's cycles and emotional balance.
- **Use:** Take as powder in warm milk or capsule form; combine with ashwagandha for full-body rejuvenation.
- **Spiritual Quality:** Known in Ayurveda as *"She who possesses a hundred husbands"* — a metaphor for boundless creative energy.

Red Clover

- **Energetic Action:** Purifying and harmonizing.
- **Benefits:** Supports lymphatic flow, clears stagnant energy, and soothes the emotional body.
- **Use:** Steep flowers for 10 minutes to make a gentle daily tonic tea.
- **Spiritual Quality:** Encourages emotional forgiveness and renewal.

Cinnamon & Cardamom

- **Energetic Action:** Warming, stimulating, heart-expanding.
- **Benefits:** Enhance circulation, uplift mood, and awaken sensual energy in a grounded way.
- **Use:** Add to teas, desserts, or morning elixirs.
- **Spiritual Quality:** Brings warmth to the waters — kindles creativity and connection.

COOLING AND SOOTHING HERBS FOR OVERACTIVE SACRAL ENERGY

If emotions feel overwhelming or desire burns excessively, use cooling, calming herbs to soothe intensity:

- **Lemon Balm** – gently relaxes nervous tension and emotional overactivity.
- **Chamomile** – softens anger, guilt, and frustration; promotes emotional safety.
- **Spearmint** – refreshes and restores emotional clarity.
- **Rose Petal** – calms the heart and reconnects sensuality with tenderness.

SACRAL BALANCING TEA BLEND

Supports creativity, hormonal balance, and emotional flow.

Ingredients:

- 1 tsp dried orange peel
- 1 tsp hibiscus
- ½ tsp cinnamon
- ½ tsp damiana (optional – for sensual energy)
- 1 tsp honey or a slice of fresh ginger

Instructions:
Steep for 5–7 minutes. Sip slowly, feeling warmth spread through your lower belly.
Repeat the affirmation:
"I receive nourishment with joy. I flow with ease. I am filled with creative life force."

HERBAL BATH FOR EMOTIONAL RELEASE

A soothing ritual bath blends herbs and intention to restore the waters of Svadhisthana.

Ingredients:

- 1 cup Epsom salts
- 1 tbsp dried rose petals
- 1 tbsp hibiscus
- 1 tsp orange peel
- A few drops of sweet orange or ylang-ylang essential oil

Instructions:
Add to warm bathwater and swirl until fragrant.
As you soak, imagine your emotional body dissolving old patterns — fear, guilt, shame — replaced by trust and pleasure. Let the water carry away what no longer serves, leaving only softness and self-acceptance.

AFFIRMATION FOR HERBAL HEALING

"Like water, I release.
Like flowers, I open.
Like herbs, I remember that healing is gentle, sensual, and sacred."

Nature Practices for the Sacral Chakra

Reconnecting to the Waters of Life

Where the Root Chakra grounds us in the earth, the **Sacral Chakra awakens us to the movement of water** — the tides, rivers, rains, and even the subtle fluids within our own bodies. To heal *Svadhisthana* is to **relearn the art of flow** — to allow nature's rhythms to mirror and regulate our own emotional and creative cycles.

In nature, everything moves in waves: the ocean's tide, the moon's pull, the change of seasons, the way light dances across water. The Sacral Chakra attunes us to this rhythm — reminding us that feeling and movement are sacred, not chaotic.

1. Connect with Natural Water

Because *Svadhisthana* is governed by the element of **Water**, immersion in or observation of water has a direct balancing effect.
Spend time near oceans, rivers, lakes, or even a small stream — anywhere that flow exists.

Practice:

- Sit by water and watch its surface.
- Match your breath to its rhythm — inhaling as waves rise, exhaling as they fall.
- Let your emotions mirror the water's movement: what flows, what stills, what reflects.

Visualization:

"As the river flows, so do I.
My emotions move freely, carrying away all that no longer
serves."

Even a **bath, shower, or bowl of water** can be a sacred tool for
flow and release when approached with reverence.

2. Moonlight Rituals and Lunar Connection

The Sacral Chakra is ruled by the **Moon**, which governs tides,
emotion, and the cycles of fertility and creativity.
Working in harmony with lunar energy helps regulate emotional
waves and creative phases.

Practice:

- Spend a few moments under the **full moon**.
- Place your hands over your womb or lower abdomen
  and breathe in the silver light.
- Whisper:

  "I honor the tides within me.
  My emotions are wise and ever-renewing."

Tip: Keep a *moon journal* to track emotional cycles,
inspiration, and intuition. Over time, you'll see how your
energy rises and falls in beautiful, predictable rhythm — just
like the moon.

3. Walking Meditation by Water

Walking near water creates a **moving meditation** — each step
syncing body, breath, and rhythm.
As you walk, focus not on distance but on feeling: the sound of
rippling water, the scent of mist, the softness of air.

Mantra:

"I flow with life.
Each step releases, each breath renews."

This simple practice realigns the emotional body and encourages intuitive movement — a natural antidote to stagnation or creative block.

4. Rain Ritual for Emotional Release

Rain cleanses both the land and the soul. Standing in gentle rain — or even visualizing it — helps release suppressed emotion and invites renewal.

Practice:

- Step outside or imagine rain falling softly over you.
- Feel it washing over your shoulders, belly, and hips.
- Whisper:

"I am cleansed. I am fluid. I am free."

Afterward, dry yourself gently and anoint your lower abdomen with a drop of orange or ylang-ylang essential oil to seal in warmth and sensual renewal.

5. Gardening and Creative Planting

Though water is the Sacral's element, plants embody the **union of earth and water** — the grounded flow that sustains life. Gardening becomes a **creative ritual** for this chakra: you nurture, tend, and bring forth beauty.

Practice:

- Water plants mindfully, visualizing orange light flowing from your hands.
- Thank the water for its life-giving energy.
- As you pour, say aloud:

"I give, I receive, I create."

6. The Dance of the Elements

To fully balance the Sacral Chakra, combine **earth (Root)** and **water (Sacral)** elements in nature practice:

- Walk barefoot on moist grass.
- Sit beside a stream with your hands in the soil.
- Float in a lake and feel the weight of your body supported by both elements.

This blending of earth and water symbolizes the **sacred union of stability and flow** — the true harmony of *Svadhisthana*.

Affirmation for Nature Connection

"The water within me flows with the rhythm of the earth.
I release, I renew, I create."

Chapter 9 – Advanced Practitioner Applications

Energetic Flow, Emotional Transmutation, and Creative Resonance

For advanced practitioners, the Sacral Chakra offers one of the most subtle yet transformative fields of work.
While the Root teaches grounding and containment, *Svadhisthana* teaches the **movement of energy — how to let emotion, pleasure, and creation flow without losing center**.

Mastery at this level means becoming fluent in emotional energy: sensing its texture, understanding its messages, and guiding its release or redirection with both skill and reverence. To work with the Sacral Chakra is to become a **translator of the waters of the soul**.

ENERGETIC DYNAMICS OF THE SACRAL FIELD

The energy of *Svadhisthana* moves like waves — rhythmic, cyclical, and alive. Unlike the linear pulse of the Root, Sacral energy flows outward in spirals and ripples.
In a client's field, this can be felt as warmth, undulation, or oscillation around the pelvis, abdomen, and lower back.

When in balance, the flow is smooth and harmonious.
When blocked, it feels sluggish, dense, or heavy — often reflecting emotional suppression or sexual trauma.

When overactive, it may feel hot, erratic, or diffuse — reflecting overstimulation or emotional flooding.

Advanced practice involves learning to match your frequency to this wave — not to control it, but to move with it.
You are not directing the river; you are guiding it back to its natural course.

ENERGETIC ASSESSMENT: READING THE WATERS

Before engaging in healing, practitioners observe the *quality of movement* in the Sacral region.

Common energy presentations include:

- **Still Water:** emotional numbness, creative stagnation, or fear of vulnerability.
- **Turbulent Water:** emotional overwhelm, mood swings, or unprocessed trauma.
- **Evaporating Water:** dissociation, burnout, or sexual disconnection.
- **Overflowing Water:** dependency, indulgence, or over-identification with desire.

Observation occurs through **Reiki scanning**, intuitive perception, or somatic attunement — noticing warmth, tingling, temperature shifts, or emotional resonance while the hands hover over the lower abdomen and hips.

EMOTIONAL TRANSMUTATION PROTOCOL

In advanced energy work, emotion is not released *out* of the client — it is **transmuted** within the field into higher vibrational frequency.
This alchemical process is guided through awareness, breath, and intention.

Protocol:

1. **Anchor the Root:** Begin by stabilizing the Root Chakra (base of spine or feet) to create containment.
2. **Activate the Flow:** Move to the Sacral region and imagine drawing a spiral of orange-gold light, turning clockwise to awaken motion.
3. **Invite the Emotion:** Allow the client to feel any arising sensation — warmth, sadness, tears, or relief.
   Say softly, "Let the water move. All emotion seeks motion."
4. **Channel Reiki or Energy Light:** Send energy into the emotional center until the sensation changes texture — often from heavy to light, cool to warm, or tight to soft.
5. **Seal with Gratitude:** Visualize the emotion dissolving into orange light, returning to the body as creative life force.
   Affirm: "All that was pain becomes power. All that was held becomes flow."

TANTRIC RESONANCE AND POLARITY HEALING

The Sacral Chakra is inherently **relational** — it governs how energy flows between self and other.
In advanced practice, healers may balance the **feminine and masculine polarities** within a client's energy body:

- **Feminine (Shakti):** receptive, feeling, creative, intuitive.
- **Masculine (Shiva):** directive, clarifying, structuring, discerning.

When one dominates, imbalance occurs — creativity without boundaries, or control without emotion.
Practitioners can work with this polarity through **dual-energy meditation**, placing one hand over the heart

(Shiva/consciousness) and one over the womb or hara (Shakti/energy).

Mantra for Integration:

"Energy and awareness, creation and consciousness, dance as one within me."

This restores harmony between emotion and direction — between feeling and purpose.

CREATIVE FIELD ACTIVATION: REAWAKENING THE FLOW OF INSPIRATION

Beyond emotional release, advanced practitioners can help clients reawaken the **creative life force** that has gone dormant due to trauma, fear, or chronic stress.

Steps for Creative Activation:

1. **Anchor the client's energy** through the feet and Root Chakra.
2. **Visualize orange light** expanding from the lower abdomen like ripples across still water.
3. **Channel Reiki or light through the hands** placed over the hips or womb area, using slow, circular movements.
4. **Invite imagery or emotion:** Ask the client to imagine a color, sound, or movement that represents their creativity.
5. **Guide expression:** Encourage a short creative act after the session — journaling, painting, singing, or dancing — to anchor the energetic awakening into form.

This converts subtle healing into embodied creation, completing the Sacral circuit.

WORKING WITH EMOTIONAL MEMORY AND ANCESTRAL IMPRINTS

Emotional memory often resides in the waters of the Sacral Chakra — particularly ancestral patterns of shame, repression, or sexual trauma.
During advanced work, practitioners may sense density or "energetic echo" in the pelvis, lower spine, or womb space.

Approach:

- Invoke the **Dai Ko Myo** symbol (or your highest attunement symbol) to bring divine light into shadowed memory.
- Hold space for emotion to surface without analysis.
- Visualize orange light infused with violet — the color of transformation — washing through the lineage field.
- Invite healing across generations with the affirmation:

  "Through me, the waters clear for those before and after."

This restores vibrational purity in the creative and reproductive energy channels.

PRACTITIONER EMBODIMENT: THE HEALER AS VESSEL OF FLOW

To effectively facilitate Sacral healing, practitioners must embody flow within themselves.
Rigid control, emotional suppression, or fear of sensual energy can unconsciously block a client's release.

Before sessions, take time to reconnect to your own body — sway, stretch, breathe into your hips, and allow emotion to move freely.

When you heal from presence, not perfection, your energy field becomes a **mirror of safety and permission**.

Mantra for Practitioners:

"I honor emotion as sacred movement.
I am the calm riverbank through which healing flows."

THE HIDDEN MASTERY OF SVADHISTHANA

At the highest level, the Sacral Chakra teaches the practitioner **emotional mastery without suppression** and **sensitivity without overwhelm**.
You become the observer and the dancer — feeling everything deeply, yet moved by none of it.

The mastery is not control, but harmony.
It is the ability to let energy move through you like water — cleansing, nourishing, and endlessly renewing.

"When emotion becomes energy, and energy becomes love, the healer and the healed are one in the same current."

Hands-On Protocols for the Sacral Chakra & Stabilizing Clients

Restoring Flow, Emotional Safety, and Energetic Balance

Working hands-on with the Sacral Chakra requires presence, sensitivity, and deep respect for boundaries.
Because *Svadhisthana* governs emotion, pleasure, and intimacy, practitioners are entering a profoundly personal energetic field.
Here, trust and safety are the gateways to transformation.

When approached with reverence, the hands become instruments of flow — **guiding energy to move, soften, and harmonize the emotional waters** that may have long been held in stillness or tension.

Client Preparation and Energetic Containment

Before addressing the Sacral directly, always create a **secure energetic container**.
The lower chakras hold the body's survival memory; if safety is not established, emotional energy may surface abruptly.

Begin each session by:

1. **Grounding the Space:**
   o Invite the client to take three deep, slow breaths.
   o State aloud: *"You are safe here. This space is sacred and held in compassion."*
2. **Connecting to the Root:**
   o Begin at the feet or base of the spine.
   o Channel Reiki or grounding energy until the field feels calm, warm, and steady.
3. **Invoking Permission:**
   o Gently inform the client that you will be working around the lower abdomen and hips, ensuring comfort and consent.
   o Allow them to guide how close or hands-off your work should be.
   o Hovering is equally effective when done with intention.

This ensures that **any emotional or sensual current that rises does so in safety** — anchored and contained within a field of trust.

Hand Placements for the Sacral Chakra

The Sacral Chakra is located approximately two inches below the navel and extends through the hips, lower back, and pelvic bowl.

Because it governs both the front (emotional expression) and back (creative power), it is ideal to treat from both directions.

Primary Positions:

1. **Front Placement (Emotional Flow):**
   - Place one hand gently over the lower abdomen, between the navel and pubic bone.
   - The second hand may rest above the navel or over the heart to connect flow with compassion.
   - This placement soothes emotional turbulence and invites trust in feeling.
2. **Back Placement (Creative Power):**
   - Place your hands over the sacrum or lower back.
   - This accesses the energetic reservoir of creative and reproductive energy.
   - A warm, pulsing sensation often indicates energy release or reactivation of flow.
3. **Hip Anchors (Balancing Polarity):**
   - Rest one hand over each hip bone.
   - This balances left and right hemispheric energy — emotional and logical, receptive and active.
   - Move your awareness like a pendulum, sensing where flow is restricted and restoring symmetry.
4. **Optional Hovering Position (Energetic Sensitivity):**
   - Hold your hands 2–3 inches above the pelvic bowl.
   - Visualize orange light swirling between your palms and the client's body.
   - This method respects privacy while still influencing deep energetic release.

Energy Movement Sequence: "Waves of Flow" Technique

This gentle flow method helps **activate the natural rhythm of energy** within the Sacral Chakra while maintaining grounding.

Steps:

1. Begin at the **Root (base of spine)** to ensure containment.
2. Move your hands slowly upward to the **Sacral region**, drawing small, circular motions in a clockwise direction.
3. Visualize orange-gold waves moving like water under your palms — steady, soothing, rhythmic.
4. As emotion or energy stirs, **mirror the rhythm** of breath — inhale with the client's rising energy, exhale to help it settle.
5. If you sense imbalance (too hot or erratic), place one hand on the sacrum and one on the solar plexus to bridge **water and fire**, calming the current.
6. End the flow by placing both hands on the **hips or knees** to ground and stabilize the energy before moving on.

Signs of Activation and Release

During Sacral work, clients may experience emotional or physical responses that indicate energetic movement:

- Gentle warmth or waves of heat in the abdomen or hips.
- Spontaneous deep breathing or sighing.
- Subtle muscle twitching or pelvic pulsation.
- Emotional expressions: tears, laughter, or a sense of relief.
- Imagery or memories surfacing from relationships or childhood.

Practitioner Note:
Maintain a steady, compassionate presence.
Do not interpret or analyze; simply hold the space.
Emotion is the body's language of release — your role is to listen through energy, not words.

Stabilizing Clients After Emotional Release

Following Sacral Chakra activation, clients often feel vulnerable, open, or euphoric.
Stabilization ensures they integrate the energy safely into their physical and emotional systems.

Stabilization Steps:

1. **Return to the Root:**
   - Place your hands at the base of the spine or feet.
   - Channel grounding Reiki until the energy feels calm and centered.
2. **Breath Integration:**
   - Invite the client to place a hand on their belly and one on their heart.
   - Guide a slow breathing pattern: *inhale into the belly, exhale from the heart.*
   - This unites love (Anahata) and emotion (Svadhisthana) in balance.
3. **Energetic Sealing:**
   - Sweep your hands lightly from head to toe, smoothing the aura.
   - Affirm softly: *"Your energy flows freely and safely within you. You are balanced, creative, and whole."*
4. **Hydration and Grounding:**
   - Encourage clients to drink water or herbal tea post-session.
   - Suggest a quiet walk in nature or gentle stretching to harmonize body and spirit.

Advanced Reiki Integration

For Reiki Masters or energy healers using symbols:

- **Sei He Ki (Emotional Harmony Symbol):** Use over the lower abdomen to balance emotion and sensuality.
- **Cho Ku Rei (Power Symbol):** Apply over the sacrum to strengthen flow without losing stability.
- **Dai Ko Myo (Master Symbol):** Use for karmic or ancestral purification, especially when emotional patterns repeat across generations.

Visualize these symbols floating like light upon the orange waters of the Sacral Chakra — activating, cleansing, and harmonizing from within.

Practitioner Awareness

The Sacral field mirrors your own emotional landscape.
If you find energy stagnating or sensations overwhelming, pause and ground.
Your breath is the bridge — inhale stability from the Root, exhale flow through the Sacral.

Remember: **you cannot guide a client through waters you fear to enter.**
The more at ease you are with emotion, sensuality, and movement, the deeper the healing becomes.

"When the healer's waters are calm, the client's storm finds its shore."

Energetic Ethics and Boundaries for Practitioners Working with the Sacral Chakra

Holding Safe Space for Emotional, Sensual, and Energetic Release

The Sacral Chakra — *Svadhisthana* — governs emotion, sensuality, and creative energy.
Because of its intimate nature, it is one of the most **delicate and sacred energy centers** to work with.
Here, practitioners must embody both compassion and clarity — becoming a vessel of presence, not projection.

Working with the Sacral is not only a technical practice; it is an ethical and spiritual responsibility.
Clients entrust you with access to their most vulnerable energetic field — the seat of pleasure, emotion, and memory.
Maintaining integrity, neutrality, and reverence ensures that the healing space remains safe, sacred, and empowering for all involved.

The Foundation of Energetic Integrity

Before addressing another's Sacral Chakra, a practitioner must first examine their own relationship with **emotion, desire, and boundaries.**
Unhealed patterns within the practitioner can unconsciously influence the session, leading to energetic entanglement or projection.

Ask yourself before each session:

- Am I grounded and emotionally clear today?
- Do I feel centered in my body and aware of my own energy?

- Can I witness emotion without absorbing it?

If the answer to any of these is "no," take time to ground and clear before proceeding.
Your energy field sets the tone — **your stability is your client's safety.**

"The healer's neutrality becomes the sanctuary where others can safely feel."

Creating Safety Through Consent and Communication

Because the Sacral Chakra governs sensitive areas of the body (lower abdomen, pelvis, hips), **clear communication and consent** are essential.
Clients must understand what to expect and feel empowered to express preferences or discomfort.

Best Practices:

1. **Explain Before Touching:**
   - Always describe where your hands will be placed or hovered.
   - Offer the option for non-contact or energetic-only work.
   - Respect all boundaries without question or hesitation.
2. **Gain Informed Consent:**
   - Use verbal agreements before each session.
   - In professional settings, consider written consent for pelvic or abdominal work.
3. **Observe Body Language:**
   - Subtle cues such as tension, shallow breathing, or shifting may indicate discomfort.
   - Pause immediately, invite feedback, and adjust your approach.
4. **Empower the Client:**

- o Remind them: *"You are always in control. If you wish to stop, change position, or shift focus, simply say so."*
- o This simple affirmation reinforces emotional safety and trust.

Maintaining Energetic Boundaries

The Sacral Chakra radiates emotional frequency — joy, grief, passion, fear, and memory can all arise here.
Without clear energetic boundaries, practitioners may absorb or mirror the client's emotions, leading to fatigue or confusion after sessions.

To maintain balance:

- **Anchor your Root Chakra** before and after every treatment.
- **Visualize a golden or violet shield** around your aura — permeable to love, impermeable to attachment.
- **State an internal intention:** *"All energy flows for the client's highest good, returning purified to Source."*
- After sessions, **cleanse your field** through salt baths, smudging, shaking, or breathwork.

Boundaries are not walls; they are **containers of compassion** — keeping both practitioner and client free within sacred structure.

Recognizing Emotional and Sensual Energy

As energy begins to move through *Svadhisthana*, clients may experience sensations that mimic emotional release or even arousal.
This is not sexual in nature — it is **the life-force reclaiming its natural current.**

Emotion and pleasure share the same energetic root; both are expressions of Shakti's movement through the body.

Practitioner Guidance:

- Stay calm, neutral, and respectful.
- Do not draw attention to the sensation unless the client initiates discussion.
- If emotion surfaces (crying, shaking, laughter), hold space silently or guide slow breathing.
- If arousal energy arises, keep your focus on grounding — move hands to hips, knees, or feet, helping the energy redistribute safely.

Never personalize or interpret these sensations. They are signs of awakening, not invitations for engagement.

Transference and Emotional Projection

The Sacral Chakra is where deep relational energies surface — including **transference** (client projecting emotions onto practitioner) and **countertransference** (practitioner responding emotionally).

Signs to watch for:

- Feeling unusually protective, attracted, or reactive toward a client.
- The client is seeking validation or emotional dependency beyond sessions.
- Sudden fatigue or emotional shifts after working with someone.

Response:
Acknowledge the dynamic internally without judgment. Reinforce professional boundaries kindly — *"Let's breathe through this energy together and ground it."*

If patterns persist, refer to another practitioner or adjust session structure.

Energetic ethics means recognizing when compassion must include distance.

Post-Session Integration and Aftercare

After deep Sacral work, clients may feel emotionally tender, euphoric, or introspective.
Guiding them in integration prevents overwhelm and encourages balance.

Offer gentle suggestions:

- Drink plenty of water — to support the element of flow.
- Journal emotions or dreams over the next 24 hours.
- Take a salt bath or spend quiet time near water.
- Avoid major decisions or sexual encounters immediately after intense energy release.

This gives the subtle body time to assimilate new frequencies.
End each session with grounding affirmations:

"You are safe in your body.
You are free to feel.
You are whole."

The Sacred Duty of the Practitioner

To work with the Sacral Chakra is to work with the river of life itself.
You are not there to control the current, but to **keep its banks strong** so that emotion can flow safely within form.

True mastery lies in presence — the quiet knowing that healing happens not because of the practitioner, but through them.

When ethics, awareness, and love unite, **the session becomes a vessel of grace**, and both practitioner and client leave more balanced, free, and luminous than before.

The Role of Svadhisthana in Remote Healing

Channeling Flow, Emotion, and Creative Connection Across Distance

While the Root Chakra grounds healing into the physical realm, the **Sacral Chakra (Svadhisthana)** governs flow — the emotional and energetic current that connects one soul to another. In remote or distant healing, Svadhisthana becomes the bridge through which **empathy, resonance, and intuitive connection** are transmitted.

Where the Root anchors, the Sacral communicates — sending energy like water traveling through an unseen stream between practitioner and client.

Energy Beyond Physical Contact

In distant healing, there is no physical touch, yet the energetic connection remains profound.
Svadhisthana governs our **capacity to feel** — not only our own emotions but the subtle emotional states of others. When a practitioner attunes to the client from afar, it is this chakra that senses, translates, and transmits energetic information.

Through the Sacral, the healer becomes a vessel for emotional empathy.
Through the Root, energy grounds into safety.
Together, they create a balanced current — **flowing yet contained, connected yet centered.**

How Svadhisthana Functions in Remote Sessions

The Sacral Chakra operates like an **energetic tuning fork**, picking up frequencies of emotion, memory, and subtle sensation. During remote sessions, this allows practitioners to perceive where emotional flow may be restricted or overactive within the client's field.

Practitioners may experience:

- Subtle warmth or pulsing in their own lower abdomen or hips.
- Emotional impressions — sadness, joy, excitement — that do not originate within themselves.
- Sensations of water-like movement, waves, or ripples through the energy field.

These sensations are not literal emotions but energetic "data." The healer's role is not to absorb or interpret them personally, but to **translate them into flow** — inviting balance, release, or calm as needed.

"In distant healing, emotion becomes vibration — felt not as story, but as movement."

Establishing Flow Without Attachment

Because the Sacral Chakra resonates with emotion and connection, remote healers must cultivate **clarity and detachment** to prevent emotional blending.
The practitioner's energy should act like a **clear river channel**, allowing Shakti to flow freely without becoming entangled in the client's current.

To maintain this clarity:

1. Begin by grounding through the Root (your own Muladhara).
2. Visualize your Sacral Chakra as a glowing orange lotus, spinning freely and clearly.
3. State the intention:

   "May energy flow through me, not from me.
   I am the vessel, not the source."

4. Allow empathy without absorption — feel the wave pass through, not stay within.

This practice protects the practitioner while allowing the healing current to travel cleanly and compassionately.

SACRAL TECHNIQUES FOR REMOTE HEALING

While every practitioner develops a personal style, several time-tested methods align especially well with Svadhisthana's fluid nature:

1. Visualization of Water Flow:
Imagine a luminous orange stream flowing from your Sacral center toward the client's.
The current carries warmth, understanding, and creative vitality — washing away tension or stagnation, restoring balance and flow.

2. Emotional Resonance Clearing:
If you sense heaviness or emotional density, send Reiki or healing intention through the water stream.
Visualize the emotion dissolving, returning to pure energy.
Whisper inwardly:

"Flow returns where it was blocked. Emotion becomes energy again."

3. Creative Transference:
The Sacral Chakra is also the seat of creation. You can channel healing through **art, sound, or movement** as part of distance work — painting, toning, or writing as an intuitive expression of the energy exchange.
What matters is not the medium, but the intention: transformation through flow.

BALANCING THE PRACTITIONER'S ENERGY AFTER SESSIONS

Because the Sacral Chakra opens empathic channels, it's essential to **close and clear the field** after each remote session. Left ungrounded, practitioners may retain fragments of the client's emotional frequency or experience fatigue.

After the session:

1. Visualize the orange current gently retracting, returning all energy to the Source.
2. Place your hands on your lower abdomen and breathe deeply.
3. Affirm:

   "All emotions return to their rightful place.
   Only peace and flow remain within me."

4. Ground through the Root — imagine roots extending from your feet deep into the earth, drawing stability back into your body.

This restores equilibrium and ensures the flow of energy continues to nourish rather than deplete.

THE GIFT OF SACRAL CONNECTION IN REMOTE HEALING

In working distantly, the Sacral Chakra teaches the practitioner one of the highest truths of energy work — **that connection transcends physical presence.**
Emotion, empathy, and intention travel effortlessly through the invisible rivers of consciousness that unite all beings.

Through Svadhisthana, the practitioner learns:

- To feel without losing center.
- To transmit love through resonance rather than effort.
- To let energy move like water — cleansing, healing, and returning all to harmony.

The secret of remote healing through the Sacral Chakra is the same as that of life itself:
When energy is allowed to flow, balance is restored.

Clearing Ancestral Fear and Karmic Imprints

Releasing Emotional Memory and Restoring the Flow of Pleasure and Creation

Just as the Root Chakra holds memories of physical survival, the **Sacral Chakra (Svadhisthana)** carries the **emotional memories** of our lineage — the unspoken feelings, suppressed desires, and inherited beliefs about pleasure, intimacy, and expression passed from generation to generation.

Where Muladhara stores the fear of death, Svadhisthana holds the fear of **feeling**. These ancestral and karmic imprints can subtly shape how we relate to our bodies, creativity, and relationships — often long before we are consciously aware of them.

Inherited Emotional Memory

Every family carries emotional signatures — energetic echoes that ripple through the generations.
When trauma, grief, or repression is left unresolved, it embeds within the collective emotional body of a lineage. These imprints are not just psychological; they are vibrational patterns that live in the **waters of the Sacral Chakra**.

You may carry ancestral memories such as:

- Shame or guilt surrounding sexuality or pleasure.
- Emotional suppression due to cultural or religious conditioning.
- Creative blockages or fear of expressing one's art or voice.
- Generational grief, loss, or betrayal within relationships.
- Cycles of emotional dependency or abandonment.

These inherited emotions move like undercurrents, shaping our instincts in love, intimacy, and self-expression until they are consciously released.

"What the ancestors could not express, we feel.
What they could not forgive, we heal."

Karmic Patterns in the Waters of Emotion

In the spiritual sense, **karma** is not punishment — it is memory seeking resolution.
The Sacral Chakra is where emotional karma plays out most visibly, as our relationships and creative cycles mirror the deeper lessons the soul is ready to face.

Recurring emotional experiences — passion followed by loss, attraction to unavailable partners, fear of vulnerability, or cycles of creative bursts and droughts — may reflect **unfinished emotional karma**.
These are not random misfortunes but invitations for emotional mastery and energetic purification.

In Tantric wisdom, water symbolizes both memory and purification.
As Kundalini rises through Svadhisthana, she stirs these karmic sediments so that they may be seen, felt, and released.
The process can feel turbulent — waves of emotion, vivid dreams, or spontaneous memories may arise — but these are signs of the water clearing.

Recognizing the Signs of Ancestral and Karmic Imprints

When ancestral emotion remains unhealed in the Sacral Chakra, it often manifests as:

- **Emotional numbness or detachment** – feeling "shut down" or unable to access joy.
- **Excessive emotional reactivity** – crying, anger, or fear that seems disproportionate to the moment.
- **Guilt surrounding pleasure or sexuality**, even when no harm has been done.
- **Repetitive relationship patterns**, often mirror ancestral stories of abandonment or betrayal.
- **Creative stagnation** – bursts of inspiration followed by sudden blocks or burnout.

The emotional body cannot flow freely while it carries another's unprocessed pain. Healing these imprints restores innocence to feeling and freedom to create.

PRACTICES FOR CLEARING ANCESTRAL FEAR AND EMOTIONAL KARMA

1. Water Ritual of Release

Since Svadhisthana is governed by the element of water, emotional release through water rituals is especially powerful.

- Sit near a body of water (or fill a bowl with saltwater).
- Speak aloud the emotions or family patterns you are ready to release — shame, silence, fear, or repression.
- As you exhale, visualize those emotions dissolving into the water, purified by its fluid wisdom.
- Whisper:

    "I release what is not mine to carry.
    May the waters remember me as free."

2. Reiki or Energy Clearing

During Reiki or hands-on healing, focus on the pelvic area, hips, and lower abdomen.
Visualize a warm orange light washing through, untangling emotional cords to ancestors or past lives.
Invite the energy to restore harmony through the entire family line.

3. Creative Transmutation

Ancestral wounds often heal through **expression**, not suppression.
Dance, paint, write, sing, or move in ways that release emotion from the body.
The act of creating becomes sacred alchemy — turning inherited pain into living art, grief into grace.

4. Forgiveness Meditation

Close your eyes, bring awareness to your lower abdomen, and
visualize your ancestors standing behind you.
With every breath, say silently:

"I honor your stories.
I bless your lessons.
I now choose freedom through love."
Feel the energy lighten as generations of unspoken emotion
dissolve into understanding.

THE HEALING FLOW RESTORED

When ancestral and karmic imprints are released, the **waters of
Svadhisthana begin to flow freely again**.
Pleasure feels safe.
Emotion becomes wisdom instead of turmoil.
Creativity awakens without resistance.

You no longer carry the grief, shame, or silence of the past —
you transform it into flow, beauty, and compassion.

This is the deeper purpose of Sacral healing:
not merely to feel pleasure or passion, but to **liberate emotion**
so that life can move again through the rivers of the soul.

"The ancestors dreamed of freedom.
You are the one who sets their dreams in motion."

RELEASING EMOTIONAL CORDS AND RESTORING CREATIVE SOVEREIGNTY
Returning to Wholeness Through Conscious Detachment and Flow

The Sacral Chakra is the seat of **connection** — the energetic bridge that allows us to bond, love, and create with others. Through this center, we form deep emotional and energetic links — with family, lovers, friends, teachers, and even creative projects. These cords are natural; they allow empathy and shared experience.

However, when attachments become imbalanced — fueled by guilt, dependency, or unhealed emotion — these cords can begin to **drain vitality** and restrict creative freedom.

Where the Root Chakra governs belonging, the Sacral governs attachment.

Healing here is not about disconnection, but about **right relationship** — learning to love without losing yourself.

Understanding Emotional Cords

Energetic cords form whenever emotional energy is exchanged. They can exist between people, places, memories, or even creative works.

Each cord carries both **affection and energy** — the invisible threads that weave us into the tapestry of life.

Healthy cords are fluid, allowing energy to flow freely in both directions.

Unhealthy cords, by contrast, feel heavy, tangled, or invasive. They may bind us to outdated emotional stories or keep us reliving pain that is no longer ours to hold.

Common examples of draining cords include:

- Remaining energetically tied to an ex-partner, even years later.
- Feeling obligated to absorb the emotions of others.
- Creative or emotional burnout from overgiving.
- Carrying guilt, resentment, or responsibility for someone else's wellbeing.
- Feeling emotionally "stuck" in past experiences or relationships.

These cords lodge most often in the **Sacral Chakra** because it governs emotion, intimacy, and exchange. Clearing them restores not isolation, but **sovereignty** — the ability to feel deeply while staying centered in one's own emotional current.

Recognizing Signs of Energetic Entanglement

When emotional cords need clearing, you may experience:

- Sudden emotional changes that don't feel like your own.
- Fatigue after interactions with certain people.
- Difficulty moving on from past relationships.
- Over-identification with another person's pain or story.
- A creative block linked to someone's expectations or criticism.

You may sense these cords physically as a weight or pressure in the lower abdomen, hips, or navel area — the energetic "tether" point of Svadhisthana.

Energetic Anatomy of Detachment

Detachment does not mean cutting people out of your life; it means releasing unhealthy dependence and energetic interference.
In the language of energy, you are not *cutting cords* (which can

leave sharp fragments), but **dissolving or releasing them** —
allowing the energy to return to its natural state of flow.

When cords dissolve:

- Compassion replaces guilt.
- Freedom replaces obligation.
- Creativity returns, unobstructed.

Through awareness and love, what once felt like emotional
bondage becomes a bridge toward self-mastery.

Releasing Emotional Cords Practice

*(To be performed with compassion and intention, not anger or
avoidance.)*

1. **Prepare the Space**
   Sit quietly, hands on your lower abdomen.
   Breathe deeply until you feel calm and centered in your
   body.
   Visualize a warm orange glow surrounding your pelvis
   and hips — the radiant waters of your Sacral Chakra.
2. **Identify the Connection**
   Bring to mind a person, memory, or situation that feels
   emotionally heavy or energetically entangled.
   Without judgment, notice where in your body you sense
   this connection — it may appear as a thread, rope, or
   light extending from your abdomen.
3. **Call in Light and Compassion**
   Visualize a gentle wave of golden-orange light washing
   through your Sacral Chakra.
   Say silently:

   "Only love and learning remain.
   All else returns to the Source."

4. **Dissolve the Cord**
   Rather than cutting or tearing, imagine the cord **softening and melting** in the light, like ice in warm water.
   Feel energy returning to both you and the other soul, purified and free.
5. **Seal the Chakra with Light**
   Once the cord has dissolved, visualize a radiant orange lotus blooming in your pelvis, spinning smoothly and filled with light.
   Whisper:

   "My emotions flow freely.
   My energy is my own.
   I love and release in peace."

The Return of Creative Sovereignty

When cords are released, creative energy naturally rebounds. The vitality that once leaked outward returns home — to the womb of your imagination, your sensuality, your joy.
You may notice renewed inspiration, deeper intimacy with yourself, and the ability to engage others from a place of choice rather than need.

This is the true essence of **creative sovereignty** —
to feel, love, and create without losing your center.

The Sacral Chakra, once burdened by the emotions of others, becomes a clear vessel for divine expression. Pleasure flows again, not as indulgence, but as **innocent participation in life's rhythm**.

"When I no longer cling, love can flow.
When I no longer fear, creativity returns.
When I no longer hold, I am held by life itself."

Cross-Referencing with TCM Meridians: Kidney and Bladder

The **Sacral Chakra (Svadhisthana)** shares a profound resonance with the **Water Element** in Traditional Chinese Medicine (TCM), which governs the **Kidney** and **Bladder meridians**. Both systems see water as the source of life, creativity, and flow — the element that carries vitality, emotion, and the power of renewal.

Where the Root Chakra represents stillness and stability, the Sacral expresses **movement and transformation** — the fluid dance of energy that sustains sensuality, reproduction, and emotional intelligence.

KIDNEY MERIDIAN – ESSENCE AND CREATIVITY

In TCM, the Kidneys are called the **"Root of Life"** because they store **Jing**, the essence of vitality inherited from our ancestors. This essence governs fertility, sexuality, and the deep inner drive to create — the same energies embodied by the Sacral Chakra.

When Kidney energy is strong, the Sacral center glows with vitality: emotions flow easily, creative energy is abundant, and sensual pleasure feels nourishing rather than depleting. When Kidney energy is weak, symptoms like exhaustion, low libido, fear of intimacy, or creative stagnation often appear.

Balancing Techniques

- Apply gentle warmth or Reiki to the lower abdomen and lower back.
- Hydrate well and rest deeply — both replenish Kidney essence.

- Work with water meditation or soft pelvic movements to restore flow.

Affirmation:

"My creative essence is replenished with every breath. I honor the sacred waters within me."

BLADDER MERIDIAN – RELEASE AND EMOTIONAL FLOW

The Bladder meridian governs the **movement and elimination of fluids**, mirroring the Sacral Chakra's role in release — both physical and emotional. Just as the bladder empties what the body no longer needs, the Sacral helps clear suppressed feelings, guilt, or shame so energy can move freely again.

When Bladder Qi stagnates, people may feel emotionally blocked, rigid, or unable to let go. When it flows, there is ease, sensual openness, and rhythmic balance in both body and mood.

Balancing Techniques

- Hydrotherapy or salt baths to cleanse emotional residue.
- Reiki or acupressure along the sacrum and lower spine to restore fluid movement.
- Deep, wave-like breathing to synchronize with the body's natural rhythm of release.

Affirmation:

"I let go with grace. My emotions flow like clear, healing waters."

THE WATER ELEMENT: THE ESSENCE OF FLOW

Both the Sacral Chakra and the Kidney–Bladder meridians are governed by **Water**, the element of adaptability, intuition, and depth. When water energy is balanced, emotion becomes wisdom, pleasure becomes sacred, and creation flows without force.

When out of balance, this same energy can stagnate — showing up as fear, emotional numbness, or overindulgence. The key is to maintain **movement with awareness** — to let energy ebb and flow naturally.

Sacral–Water Integration Practice

- Visualize water swirling in your pelvis, glowing with orange light.
- As you breathe, imagine this water cleansing old emotions and replenishing your essence.
- Feel it flowing upward into the heart and downward into the earth, connecting heaven, body, and spirit.

Affirmation:

"I am fluid, creative, and whole. My energy flows freely through the waters of life."

Flow Synchronization: Aligning Practitioner and Client

When working with the **Sacral Chakra (Svadhisthana)**, the practitioner's own emotional flow and energetic openness profoundly influence the client. This chakra governs *connection, emotion, and rhythm* — it naturally entrains to the subtle emotional tone of others. If the practitioner is relaxed, centered, and in emotional harmony, the client's energy begins to flow in resonance. But if the practitioner is tense, guarded, or emotionally stagnant, that imbalance can unconsciously transfer to the client.

Flow synchronization is therefore essential when facilitating Sacral Chakra healing. It aligns practitioner and client into a shared field of emotional safety, creative rhythm, and trust — the foundations of healing at Svadhisthana.

Why Synchronization Matters

- **Emotional Resonance:** The Sacral Chakra responds through feeling, not logic. When two energy fields meet in empathy and attunement, emotional release becomes effortless.
- **Safety in Vulnerability:** This chakra governs intimacy and trust. Clients sense when the practitioner's field is emotionally stable, allowing them to open safely.
- **Fluid Energy Exchange:** A synchronized flow prevents emotional overwhelm or stagnation during sessions, keeping energy moving in balance between practitioner and client.

Practitioner Preparation

1. **Center in Your Own Flow**
   Before beginning, breathe deeply into your lower abdomen.
   Visualize a pool of warm, orange light beneath your navel.
   Whisper silently:

   "I am fluid, calm, and connected to life's rhythm."

2. **Emotional Check-In**
   Notice your own emotional tone — are you calm,

rushed, heavy, or excited?
Allow any feelings to surface and flow through your
breath before entering the session.

3. **Set the Intention**
As you step into the healing space, affirm:

"May my presence invite ease, trust, and creative flow."

Synchronization Techniques

1. **Shared Rhythmic Breathing**
   - Invite the client to place one hand on their lower belly.
   - Breathe together, inhaling for 4 counts, exhaling for 4 counts.
   - Imagine the breath creating gentle waves through the pelvis — rising, falling, harmonizing.
2. **Mirroring Energy Flow**
   - As you sense the client's breathing and movement, subtly match their rhythm.
   - This creates kinesthetic empathy — a shared energetic dance that allows emotion to surface safely.
3. **Energetic Linking**
   - Visualize a ribbon of orange light connecting your Sacral Chakra to the client's.
   - See this ribbon moving fluidly, like a current of water between two lakes — exchanging calm, creative energy.
4. **Closing Synchronization**
   - Near the end, visualize both your Sacral centers glowing brightly, then gently disconnecting the orange ribbon.
   - Encourage the client to take several slow breaths and notice the warmth or movement in their hips and abdomen.

Key Considerations

- **Boundaries with Compassion:**
  Flow synchronization is *attunement*, not emotional absorption. Stay aware of your own emotional edges and release what is not yours after the session.
- **Authenticity Over Technique:**
  Clients feel sincerity more than skill. A practitioner who is comfortable with their own emotions allows others to feel safe exploring theirs.
- **Integration Practices:**
  After the session, invite clients to ground the emotional work — through water, gentle stretching, journaling, or creative expression (like painting, movement, or music).

Practitioner's Affirmation Before Synchronization

"I am calm, fluid, and present.
My emotions flow freely and clearly.
Through empathy and rhythm, I invite healing.

Practitioner Energy Hygiene After Flow Work

Working with the **Sacral Chakra (Svadhisthana)** engages powerful emotional and creative energies — both the client's and the practitioner's. Because this chakra governs connection, empathy, and intimacy, it is easy for practitioners to unconsciously absorb emotional residue or carry energetic "imprints" from sessions.
Maintaining **energetic hygiene** after Sacral work ensures that your field remains clear, vibrant, and flowing — preventing fatigue, emotional heaviness, or creative stagnation.

WHY ENERGY HYGIENE MATTERS

- **Emotional Boundaries:** The Sacral Chakra is the center of empathy. Without conscious clearing, practitioners may internalize clients' emotional states.
- **Fluid Balance:** Excess Sacral energy can cause mood swings or overstimulation, while depletion can leave you uninspired or disconnected.
- **Professional Longevity:** Regular cleansing allows you to maintain emotional neutrality and creative vitality across multiple sessions or clients.

POST-SESSION RESET PRACTICES

1. **Water Purification Ritual**
   After each session, wash your hands and wrists under running water while visualizing orange light washing away emotional residue.
   Say silently:

   "I release what is not mine. I return to my own flow."
   When possible, take a brief shower or immerse your feet in water to complete the cleansing.

2. **Pelvic Breath Release**
   Sit comfortably and place your hands over your lower abdomen.
   Inhale through the nose, drawing breath into the belly.
   Exhale through the mouth with a soft sigh, imagining excess energy flowing out through the exhale.
   Repeat 3–5 times to restore emotional equilibrium.

3. **Creative Clearing**
   Engage in a short act of spontaneous creativity —
   humming, sketching, or swaying your hips gently.
   This moves any lingering energy through expression, returning it to motion rather than containment.

4. **Smudging or Aromatic Renewal**
   Use cleansing herbs or essential oils like **sweet orange**, **ylang-ylang**, or **clary sage** to refresh the treatment space and your aura.
   Wave the smoke or mist around your lower abdomen and hips while affirming:

   "Only clarity, compassion, and flow remain."

5. **Reconnection to the Root**
   To stabilize after deep Sacral work, bring attention to the Root Chakra.
   Visualize red light beneath the orange of the Sacral — firm, steady, grounding.
   This step prevents emotional drift and ensures balance between flow and foundation.

LONG-TERM MAINTENANCE

- **Hydration:** Drink plenty of water to keep energy circulating.
- **Movement:** Dance, stretch, or walk to prevent stagnation in the hips and lower spine.
- **Emotional Check-Ins:** Journal or meditate regularly on how your body feels after sessions. If heaviness or exhaustion persists, dedicate a full day to rest and energetic clearing.
- **Energetic Baths:** Once a week, soak in a bath with Epsom salt and a few drops of orange or jasmine oil. Visualize emotional tension dissolving into the water.

PRACTITIONER'S CLOSING AFFIRMATION

"I honor my energy as sacred.
I release all that is not mine.
My emotions flow freely, my creativity renews, and my body rests in balance."

Chapter 10 –
Transformation Through
Svadhisthana

Case Studies: Reclaiming Emotion,
Creativity, and Pleasure

The **Sacral Chakra (Svadhisthana)** is the center of feeling, pleasure, and creative flow. Transformation at this level is rarely about survival — it is about *aliveness*. When Svadhisthana heals, numbness gives way to vitality, suppression to expression, and shame to self-acceptance.

The following case studies illustrate how balancing the Sacral Chakra can restore emotional movement, revitalize creativity, and awaken sensual confidence. These examples demonstrate that true healing at Svadhisthana involves not just feeling again, but *trusting* emotion as a sacred guide.

CASE STUDY 1 – FROM EMOTIONAL NUMBNESS TO FLOW

Client Presentation:
A 42-year-old woman reported emotional detachment following years of caretaking for others. She described herself as "functioning but flat" — unable to cry, laugh, or feel excitement. Physically, she experienced pelvic tightness, menstrual irregularities, and low libido.

Assessment:
Energetic evaluation revealed stagnation around the pelvis and lower abdomen. The Sacral Chakra felt dense, with weak flow into both hips. The Root was stable, but the emotional current of Svadhisthana was blocked by long-term suppression of feeling.

Therapeutic Process:

- **Reiki & Breathwork:** Sessions began with gentle hands-on healing over the sacrum, followed by wave-like breathing to invite fluid motion.
- **Water Element Meditation:** The client was guided to visualize warm, orange light flowing through the pelvis like a river.
- **Expressive Practices:** She was encouraged to journal her emotions without judgment and engage in spontaneous dance for 10 minutes daily.

Outcome:
Within three weeks, the client reported spontaneous tears, laughter, and renewed connection to her body. Her cycle normalized, and she described feeling "alive again."
Transformation: Emotional numbness dissolved into flow; she rediscovered sensitivity as a strength rather than a burden.

CASE STUDY 2 – HEALING CREATIVE BLOCK AND SEXUAL SHAME

Client Presentation:
A 35-year-old artist sought help for creative stagnation and guilt surrounding sexual expression. Raised in a strict environment, he associated pleasure with wrongdoing. Though financially successful, he described feeling "dry inside."

Assessment:
The Sacral Chakra was over-controlled — bright but

constricted. Energy rose easily into the Solar Plexus (willpower) but bypassed the Sacral's emotional depth. Suppressed desire and creative fear created energetic rigidity through the lower abdomen.

Therapeutic Process:

- **Mantra Work:** The bija mantra *VAM* was introduced, helping him reconnect sound and vibration to the pelvic area.
- **Aromatherapy:** Sweet orange and ylang-ylang essential oils were used to evoke warmth and joy.
- **Reframing Pleasure:** Guided meditation helped him reinterpret pleasure as *presence*, not indulgence.
- **Somatic Practice:** Gentle hip-circling and breath synchronization restored movement through the pelvis.

Outcome:
Creative energy returned within two sessions. He began painting daily and reported increased ease in emotional and sexual expression. The guilt that once constrained him transformed into reverence for pleasure as a life force.
Transformation: Shame transmuted into inspiration; the creative and sensual currents merged into one sacred flow.

CASE STUDY 3 – RESTORING EMOTIONAL INTIMACY AFTER TRAUMA

Client Presentation:
A 50-year-old survivor of past relationship trauma experienced difficulty with intimacy and a deep fear of vulnerability. She often dissociated during emotional closeness, describing herself as "watching life from outside."

Assessment:
Both the Root and Sacral Chakras were underactive, though the Heart was open. Emotion flowed upward in bursts but

disconnected from the body below. The client's energy field showed tension at the sacrum and solar plexus, indicating fear of losing control.

Therapeutic Process:

- **Safety First:** Sessions began by anchoring into the Root to ensure stability.
- **Reiki and Flow Synchronization:** Gentle, rhythmic touch and synchronized breathing reconnected body awareness with emotion.
- **Water Ritual:** The client was guided to take weekly ritual baths infused with rose and clary sage, focusing on self-touch as healing rather than defense.
- **Affirmation Practice:**

  "It is safe to feel. My emotions flow with love and trust."

Outcome:
After several months, she described feeling warmth in her belly for the first time in years. Emotional intimacy became less frightening, and she re-entered relationships with a sense of inner safety.
Transformation: The body became a home for emotion again; vulnerability shifted from danger to sacred openness.

KEY LESSONS FROM SVADHISTHANA HEALING

1. **Flow Restores Life:** When emotion is allowed to move, vitality naturally returns. Stagnation is not healed by control, but by permission.
2. **Pleasure is Sacred:** When viewed with consciousness, pleasure connects us to divine joy rather than distraction or shame.

3. **Creativity Heals the Emotional Body:** Artistic or sensual expression allows repressed emotion to transmute into beauty.
4. **Safety Enables Surrender:** Healing the Sacral always depends on the foundation of a grounded Root — emotional freedom can only exist where the body feels secure.

PRACTITIONER'S REFLECTION

Transformation at the Sacral Chakra is a return to life's rhythm. The practitioner's role is to *midwife emotion* — to create the conditions where energy can flow without fear or resistance. Each client's awakening may look different: tears, laughter, art, sensuality, or silence. Yet beneath every story is the same truth: **When emotion moves, the soul breathes again.**

Chapter 11 – Reflection & Integration

Daily Self-Care Rituals for Sacral Strength

Healing the **Sacral Chakra (Svadhisthana)** is not a one-time event — it is a rhythm, a relationship with flow.
Where the Root teaches stability, the Sacral teaches movement. Its strength lies in flexibility: the ability to feel deeply without drowning, to express freely without losing center, to move through life with grace and receptivity.

Daily self-care at the level of Svadhisthana means cultivating awareness of how energy flows through emotion, pleasure, and creativity. These practices help you maintain that current — balanced, warm, and alive.

1. Morning Flow Activation

Begin each day by awakening the body's waters.

- **Movement:** Before checking your phone or speaking, spend 5 minutes swaying your hips, circling your pelvis, or practicing gentle cat-cow movements.
- **Breath:** Inhale deeply into your lower abdomen; exhale through the mouth with a soft sigh.
- **Intention:** Whisper,

  "Today I allow energy to move through me with ease and joy."

This morning ritual keeps emotional energy from stagnating and invites pleasure into ordinary moments.

2. Emotional Check-In Journal

The Sacral Chakra thrives on honest feeling. Suppression blocks flow, but naming emotions restores movement.
Each day, pause and write:

- *What am I feeling right now?*
- *Where do I feel it in my body?*
- *What might this emotion need from me?*

Do not analyze — simply allow emotion to have voice. Over time, this practice builds emotional intelligence and safety within the self.

3. Water Rituals

Because Svadhisthana is governed by the element of **water**, daily contact with water rejuvenates its current.

- **Morning rinse:** As you shower, imagine the water washing through your lower abdomen, carrying away yesterday's emotions.
- **Evening soak:** Add a few drops of orange, jasmine, or ylang-ylang essential oil to your bath, visualizing warm orange light enveloping your hips and lower belly.
- **Hydration:** Sip water consciously throughout the day — not just to quench thirst, but to remind yourself that energy flows best when nourished.

4. Pleasure Practice

Healthy pleasure is sacred, not indulgent.
Once a day, engage in a small act that feels good *without guilt*: savor a piece of fruit, listen to music that moves your body,

wear something soft, stretch slowly, or dance.
Pleasure teaches the nervous system that safety and joy can coexist — the essence of Sacral strength.

5. Creative Expression Time

Svadhisthana energy is inherently creative. To keep it balanced, expression must match emotion.

- Paint, cook, sing, write, garden, decorate — anything that channels inner feeling into outer form.
- Choose a creative outlet that has no goal other than enjoyment.
- If frustration arises, let it move through movement or sound rather than suppression.

Creativity is how the Sacral purifies itself — emotion becomes art, and energy becomes beauty.

6. Evening Reflection & Stillness

At day's end, lie down or sit with one hand on your lower abdomen.
Breathe slowly, allowing the day's emotions to settle like silt in clear water.
Ask yourself:

- *Did I allow myself to feel today?*
- *Where did I resist flow?*
- *What moment brought me joy?*

Acknowledge, forgive, release.
Finish with the affirmation:

"I am fluid, balanced, and alive. I honor my emotions as sacred."

7. Weekly Flow Reset

Once per week, dedicate time to a deeper ritual of Sacral renewal. Options include:

- A creative day without deadlines or screens.
- A movement class (dance, yoga, tai chi) focused on fluidity.
- A ritual bath with crystals like carnelian or orange calcite.
- Journaling to release guilt, shame, or emotional residue. These moments allow Svadhisthana to reset, ensuring emotional balance and creative vitality for the week ahead.

Integration Insight

Sacral strength is not rigidity — it is adaptability.
When this chakra is balanced, you respond to life like water: yielding yet powerful, reflective yet unstoppable.
Through consistent daily rituals of movement, emotion, and creative joy, you turn your body into the temple of flow — where pleasure is prayer, feeling is wisdom, and creation is devotion.

Journaling Prompts for the Sacral Chakra

Embodying Flow, Emotion, and Creative Power

The **Sacral Chakra (Svadhisthana)** thrives on movement, honesty, and emotional permission.
Journaling is one of the most potent tools for healing this energy center because it transforms feeling into expression — turning emotion into motion.
These prompts are designed to help you rediscover joy, embrace sensuality, release guilt, and nurture your creative pulse.

1. Emotional Awareness

- What emotions do I tend to suppress or hide from others?
- What do I fear might happen if I let myself feel fully?
- How does my body react when emotion begins to rise — do I tighten, numb, or allow it to move?
- In what moments do I feel most emotionally alive?

2. Pleasure and Sensuality

- What does healthy pleasure mean to me?
- When was the last time I experienced pleasure without guilt or self-judgment?
- Are there areas of my life where I equate pleasure with shame or fear?
- How can I create a safe, sacred relationship with my sensual energy?

3. Creativity and Expression

- What creative activity makes me lose track of time?
- How do I express emotion through art, movement, or voice?
- What blocks my creativity — fear of failure, perfectionism, or lack of permission?
- If my creative energy were water, what would it need right now — containment, flow, direction, or rest?

4. Relationships and Emotional Exchange

- How do I tend to connect with others: through emotion, logic, or action?
- Do I allow intimacy easily, or do I fear being seen too deeply?
- What patterns repeat in my emotional or romantic relationships?

- Where do I give too much or hold back too tightly?

5. Healing and Release

- What past experiences taught me to suppress emotion or pleasure?
- Is there an old guilt or memory that still lingers in my body?
- How can I release that story with compassion rather than judgment?
- What would forgiveness — for myself or another — feel like in my body?

6. Flow and Trust

- Where in my life do I resist change or hold onto control?
- What would it mean to trust life's flow, even when it feels uncertain?
- How can I bring more spontaneity and play into my daily routine?
- If I allowed emotion to move freely, how might my life feel different?

7. Sacred Affirmations

After reflecting, close your journaling practice with one or more of these affirmations:

"I honor my emotions as divine messengers."

"My body is a sacred vessel of pleasure and creativity."

"I allow myself to feel fully and flow freely."

"I release guilt and open to joy."

"My creativity is infinite, fluid, and alive."

Integration Note

Journaling for the Sacral Chakra is not about perfection or
answers — it's about *movement*.
Let your handwriting flow like water.
If tears come, let them cleanse.
If laughter rises, let it ripple through you.
Every word is a wave returning you to your natural rhythm — a
living reminder that emotional flow is the language of the soul.

GUIDED EXERCISE: AWAKENING THE WATERS OF SVADHISTHANA

The **Sacral Chakra** is the seat of your emotions, creativity,
sensuality, and connection to pleasure.
Where the Root grounds you to the earth, the Sacral invites you
to *flow* — to move, feel, and trust life's rhythm again.
This guided exercise awakens the gentle current of energy
within your lower abdomen and pelvis, helping you restore
balance between control and surrender, stillness and movement,
containment and expression.

Preparation

Find a quiet space where you can sit or lie comfortably.
Have a small bowl of water, an orange or coral candle, or soft
music playing if you wish.
Close your eyes.
Place one hand on your lower abdomen, just below the navel,
and the other hand over your heart.

Take a few deep breaths —
Inhaling through the nose, exhaling through the mouth with a
soft sigh.
Allow your body to settle into stillness, but your energy to
begin to move.

Step 1: The Breath of Flow

Breathe deeply into your lower belly.
Feel your abdomen expand gently with each inhale, and
contract naturally with each exhale.
Imagine that your breath is creating small ripples on the surface
of a still lake inside you.
Each breath smooths the waters, releasing tension and
awakening warmth in your belly.

Say softly to yourself:

"With each breath, I awaken the flow of life within me."

Continue for several breaths, letting the waves of breath expand
and recede.

Step 2: The Light of Emotion

Visualize a **soft orange light** glowing within your lower
abdomen.
This light shimmers like sunlight dancing on moving water.
With each inhale, the light brightens.
With each exhale, it expands, filling your hips, pelvis, and
lower back with gentle warmth.

As the light grows, imagine it flowing through you like a warm
river — carrying away old emotions, guilt, or creative blocks.
You may see these emotions as darker ripples dissolving into
the glowing orange current.

Whisper:

"I allow emotion to move through me freely. I release what no
longer serves me."

Step 3: The Dance of Energy

Gently begin to move your body — small circles with your hips, or subtle rocking if lying down.
Feel the movement guided by your breath, not your mind.
This motion activates the Sacral waters, connecting emotion and physical flow.

As you move, imagine the orange light pulsing rhythmically with your breath — a gentle wave of life force energy moving through your entire being.

Repeat inwardly:

"I am fluid. I am open. I am the rhythm of creation."

Step 4: The Heart Connection

Now bring awareness to your heart while keeping your lower abdomen warm and alive.
See a green light in your heart and an orange light in your sacral center.
On your next breath, visualize these lights connecting — a flowing stream of energy moving between love (heart) and emotion (sacral).

Feel love descending from your heart into your belly, and creativity rising from your belly into your heart.
Together they form a radiant current of compassion and passion — love in motion.

Whisper:

"My emotions are guided by love. My creativity flows with compassion."

Step 5: Affirmation and Stillness

Now let the movement come to rest.
Breathe gently and feel your whole lower body glowing in
warmth and ease.
You are relaxed, yet vibrant — calm, yet alive.

Say quietly or aloud:

"I am a vessel of flow, creation, and joy.
My emotions are sacred.
My pleasure is divine.
My creativity is endless."

Remain here for a few moments, simply breathing and allowing
your inner waters to settle into harmony.

When ready, open your eyes and stretch.
Take a sip of water to anchor the element within you.

Integration

This exercise can be practiced daily or weekly, especially when
you feel emotionally blocked, creatively dry, or disconnected
from pleasure.
Over time, the movement of breath and visualization retrains
the body to associate emotion with *safety*, not fear — allowing
energy to circulate freely through Svadhisthana and beyond.

The more you honor your emotions and creative urges, the more
your Sacral Chakra becomes a river of radiant life force —
flowing gracefully between the earth and your heart.

Chapter 12 – Quick Reference Toolkit

Sacral Chakra (Svadhisthana)

THE SEAT OF FLOW, EMOTION, AND CREATIVE POWER

Core Overview

Aspect	Description
Sanskrit Name	*Svadhisthana* — "One's Own Place" or "Seat of the Self"
Element	Water 🌊 (fluidity, adaptability, cleansing)
Color	Orange
Location	Lower abdomen, pelvis, hips, reproductive organs
Gland/Organs	Ovaries, testes, bladder, kidneys, uterus, lower digestive tract
Sense	Taste
Bija (Seed) Mantra	**VAM** (pronounced "vahm")
Symbol	Six-petaled lotus with a crescent moon inside

Aspect	Description
Primary Themes	Emotion, pleasure, creativity, sensuality, flow, relationships, adaptability
Core Lesson	To feel and express emotions freely; to honor pleasure as sacred; to flow with change
Shadow Energy	Guilt, shame, repression, emotional instability, creative block, addiction, codependency

BALANCED SVADHISTHANA ENERGY

- Emotional openness and honesty
- Healthy pleasure and sensual awareness
- Creative inspiration and self-expression
- Fluidity and adaptability in life
- Ability to nurture self and others
- Balanced relationships and healthy boundaries

Mantra:

"I honor the sacred flow of life within me."

SIGNS OF IMBALANCE

Underactive Sacral Chakra

- Emotional numbness or repression
- Low libido or disinterest in pleasure
- Creative stagnation or lack of motivation
- Difficulty expressing feelings
- Fear of intimacy or change

Overactive Sacral Chakra

- Emotional overreactions or drama
- Addiction to pleasure or escapism
- Overdependence in relationships
- Sexual compulsion or instability
- Lack of emotional boundaries

BALANCING PRACTICES

Physical

- Hip-opening yoga poses (Bound Angle, Goddess, Pigeon)
- Pelvic breathing or wave breathing
- Dancing, swimming, tai chi, or fluid movement

Emotional

- Journaling feelings daily
- Practicing vulnerability and self-forgiveness
- Creative expression through art, sound, or writing

Energetic

- Chant the bija mantra **VAM** for 3–9 minutes
- Reiki hand positions over the lower abdomen and hips
- Visualization of orange light pulsing gently like a tide

Spiritual

- Moon meditations and water rituals
- Tantric awareness of pleasure as devotion
- Heart–Sacral connection meditation

AROMATHERAPY ALLIES

Oil	Qualities	Use
Sweet Orange	Uplifting, joyful, creative	Diffuse to awaken inspiration
Ylang-Ylang	Sensual, softening, heart-opening	Add to bath or massage oil
Sandalwood	Sacred, grounding, harmonizing	Apply (diluted) to lower abdomen
Jasmine	Feminine empowerment, passion	Wear on pulse points during creative work
Clary Sage	Emotional release, hormonal balance	Inhale during meditation or reflection

Affirmation:

"I allow pleasure, creativity, and emotion to flow freely through me."

CRYSTAL COMPANIONS

Crystal	Qualities	How to Use
Carnelian	Creativity, vitality, confidence	Place on lower abdomen or wear as jewelry
Orange Calcite	Joy, movement, emotional cleansing	Meditate with or carry daily
Moonstone	Feminine energy, intuition, emotional rhythm	Hold during full or new moon rituals

Crystal	Qualities	How to Use
Sunstone	Pleasure, playfulness, radiant confidence	Keep near workspace for motivation
Amber	Warmth, vitality, and cleansing	Wear or use in crystal grids for emotional release

Charging Tip:
To align with the element of **water**, gently rinse your Sacral crystals in running water or place them near a flowing stream or bowl of water under moonlight.
As you do, say:

"I charge you with flow, joy, and creative light."

NUTRITION & FOOD THERAPY

- **Supportive Foods:** Oranges, mangoes, melons, peaches, carrots, pumpkin, sweet potatoes
- **Hydration:** Drink pure water, herbal teas (hibiscus, rooibos), coconut water
- **Spices:** Cinnamon, vanilla, nutmeg, cardamom
- **Symbolic Food Ritual:** Eat one orange food per day consciously — feel its color, texture, and taste as nourishment for your creative center.

SOUND & FREQUENCY HEALING

- **Bija Mantra:** VAM
- **Musical Key:** D
- **Frequency:** 288 Hz or 417 Hz (solfeggio frequency for emotional clearing)
- **Instruments:** Flowing water sounds, ocean drums, chimes, singing bowls tuned to D

Affirmation to Pair:

"My emotions are balanced. My creativity is infinite. My joy is sacred."

QUICK ENERGY RESET

1. Sit comfortably with your spine tall.
2. Inhale into your lower belly for 4 counts.
3. Exhale slowly for 6 counts, imagining orange light expanding outward.
4. Whisper:

   "I trust the flow of my emotions."

5. Place your hand on your lower abdomen, visualizing calm waves moving through you.

Within 2–3 minutes, you'll feel warmth, release, and reconnection to your inner rhythm.

INTEGRATION REMINDER

Healing Svadhisthana is not about controlling your emotions — it's about **trusting their flow**.
When you allow yourself to feel deeply, express freely, and create joyfully, you restore the sacred rhythm that connects body, heart, and soul.

Let your daily rituals, movement, and creativity become offerings to the river of life within you.
You are meant not only to survive — but to *feel, flow, and flourish.*

Conclusion: Living Through the Sacral

The **Sacral Chakra** is the song of life made fluid — the current that turns stillness into movement, instinct into emotion, and existence into creation.
Where the Root teaches us to belong to the earth, the Sacral reminds us to *dance upon it.*

To live through Svadhisthana is to remember that feeling is sacred.
Every emotion, from joy to sorrow, is the language of your soul speaking through the body.
Every creative impulse is a spark of divinity seeking form.
Every act of pleasure, when infused with awareness, becomes a prayer of gratitude for being alive.

The lesson of the Sacral is not indulgence, but **permission** — the permission to feel, to move, to create, to connect.
When we deny emotion, we dam the river; when we allow it, life flows again.
When we repress desire, it becomes shadow; when we honor it, it becomes devotion.
The Sacral invites us to find beauty in vulnerability, to trust the tides of change, and to surrender to the rhythm of becoming.

When Svadhisthana is balanced, life moves through us effortlessly:

- We express emotion without fear.
- We create without hesitation.

- We love without clinging.
- We feel without shame.

From this flow, creativity blossoms, relationships deepen, and joy becomes our natural state.
The world around us begins to mirror the harmony within.

But perhaps the greatest wisdom of the Sacral Chakra is its invitation to live as *water lives*:
To bend without breaking.
To move without losing form.
To cleanse, refresh, and return — again and again — to the source of joy within.

You do not need to chase pleasure; you need only to open to it.
You do not need to seek creativity; you need only to stop resisting its flow.
You do not need to control emotion; you need only to feel it, let it rise, and let it fall, knowing it will always bring you home to yourself.

As you close this book, place your hand on your lower belly.
Breathe softly.
Feel the gentle pulse of life moving within you — a reminder that energy, emotion, and love are never separate. They are one continuous river, flowing from your root to your heart and beyond.

This is the gift of Svadhisthana:
to live not just grounded, but alive;
not just surviving, but *feeling*;
not just existing, but *creating*.

Let your life be your art.
Let your emotions be your guide.
And let your body be the sacred vessel through which the Divine learns to flow.

SACRAL CHAKRA BENEDICTION: THE BLESSING OF FLOW

Beloved seeker of feeling and form,
You have journeyed through the waters of creation —
where emotion becomes language,
and movement becomes prayer.

May your heart remember what your body already knows:
that to feel is not weakness, but wisdom.
That every tear, every sigh, every shiver of joy
is the Divine whispering, *"I am here."*

May your emotions move freely,
like rivers finding their way to the sea.
May your creativity rise like dawnlight on calm waters,
illuminating all you touch with warmth and beauty.

May you release guilt and shame into the current,
trusting that healing flows where resistance ends.
May your pleasure be sacred,
your body a temple of joy,
your expression a hymn to life itself.

And when life changes — as it always will —
may you flow with grace,
anchored in love, guided by the quiet rhythm within.

Remember:
You are the artist and the canvas,
the tide and the moon that pulls it.
You are not separate from creation —
you *are* creation, made holy through feeling.

So dance, beloved soul,
dance in the waters of Svadhisthana.
Let your laughter ripple through existence,

let your love paint the air with color,
and let your spirit remember this truth:

You are the river,
You are the ocean,
You are the flow of life made divine.

Bibliography

CLASSICAL & YOGIC SOURCES

- Feuerstein, Georg. *The Yoga Tradition: Its History, Literature, Philosophy, and Practice.* Hohm Press, 2001.
- Avalon, Arthur (Sir John Woodroffe). *The Serpent Power: The Secrets of Tantric and Shaktic Yoga.* Dover Publications, 1974.
- Swami Sivananda. *The Chakras.* Divine Life Society, 1994.
- Easwaran, Eknath (trans.). *The Upanishads.* Nilgiri Press, 2007.
- Vivekananda, Swami. *Raja Yoga.* Advaita Ashrama, 1896. *(Optional addition — foundational for chakra and kundalini teachings.)*

CHAKRA & ENERGY HEALING WORKS

- Judith, Anodea. *Wheels of Life: A User's Guide to the Chakra System.* Llewellyn Publications, 1987.
- Myss, Caroline. *Anatomy of the Spirit.* Harmony Books, 1996.
- Brennan, Barbara Ann. *Hands of Light: A Guide to Healing Through the Human Energy Field.* Bantam, 1988.
- Sills, Franklyn. *Foundations in Craniosacral Biodynamics: The Breath of Life and Fundamental Skills.* North Atlantic Books, 2012.
- Leadbeater, C. W. *The Chakras.* Quest Books, 1972. *(Optional addition — influential in Western chakra interpretation.)*

REIKI & SPIRITUAL HEALING

- Takata, Hawayo. *Reiki: Hawayo Takata's Story*. Reiki Alliance, 1998.
- Petter, Frank Arjava. *This Is Reiki: Transformation of Body, Mind and Soul from the Origins to the Practice*. Lotus Press, 2012.
- Rand, William Lee. *Reiki: The Healing Touch*. Vision Publications, 1991.
- Santego, Constance. *Reiki Wisdom Series*. Maximillian Enterprises, 2024–. *(Include this if you're listing your own foundational Reiki series.)*

CROSS-CULTURAL & MYSTICAL REFERENCES

- Halevi, Z'ev ben Shimon. *Kabbalah: Tradition of Hidden Knowledge*. Thames & Hudson, 1991.
- Hanh, Thich Nhat. *Peace Is Every Step*. Bantam, 1992.
- Ibn Arabi. *Journey to the Lord of Power*. Inner Traditions, 1981.
- Underhill, Evelyn. *Mysticism: A Study in the Nature and Development of Spiritual Consciousness*. Dover Publications, 2002.
- Campbell, Joseph. *The Power of Myth*. Doubleday, 1988. *(Optional — bridges mythic and archetypal perspectives on energy and emotion.)*

MODERN SCIENCE & RESEARCH

- McCraty, Rollin, et al. *Science of the Heart: Exploring the Role of the Heart in Human Performance*. HeartMath Institute, 2015.
- Childre, Doc, and Howard Martin. *The HeartMath Solution*. HarperOne, 1999.
- Pert, Candace B. *Molecules of Emotion: The Science Behind Mind-Body Medicine*. Scribner, 1997.

- Lipton, Bruce H. *The Biology of Belief.* Hay House, 2005.
- Dispenza, Joe. *Becoming Supernatural: How Common People Are Doing the Uncommon.* Hay House, 2017. *(Optional modern neuro-energy link.)*

ADDITIONAL RESOURCES

- Eden, Donna. *Energy Medicine.* TarcherPerigee, 2008.
- Osho. *The Book of Secrets: 112 Meditations to Discover the Mystery Within.* St. Martin's Griffin, 1998.
- Chopra, Deepak. *Quantum Healing.* Bantam, 1989.
- Hay, Louise. *You Can Heal Your Life.* Hay House, 1984. *(Optional — emotional–physical correspondences.)*

Message From The Author

By the time you've reached this third book in the *Chakra 101* series, you've already walked through the sacred gateways of **love** and **safety**.
You have opened the Heart, learned to root into the Earth — and now, you stand before the waters of **emotion and creation**, ready to move, feel, and flow.

The **Sacral Chakra** invites us into the most intimate relationship of all — the one we have with our feelings, our bodies, and our creative essence.
Here, healing becomes fluid.
Love becomes movement.
Spirit becomes sensual.

Where the Root taught stability and belonging, the Sacral teaches surrender and expression. It reminds us that emotion is not something to control but something to listen to; that pleasure is not indulgence but reverence; and that creativity is the soul's way of making beauty out of experience.

Each wave of feeling, each spark of inspiration, carries divine intelligence. When we learn to trust that flow — to let emotion, desire, and imagination dance together — we begin to live as artists of our own lives.

This book is your invitation to reclaim that artistry.
To honor your emotions as sacred currents of energy.
To express without fear.
To find joy in embodiment, and power in vulnerability.

As you explore these pages, may you allow yourself to soften where you once held tight, to feel where you once resisted, and to create where you once hesitated.

May the waters of your being flow clear again — carrying you home to yourself.

With love, gratitude, and the joy of your unfolding,
Dr. Constance Santego

About the Author

Dr. Constance Santego, Ph.D., DNM, is an award-winning author, teacher, and natural medicine doctor who has dedicated

more than 25 years to the study and practice of energy healing. A Grand Reiki Master and founder of multiple wellness and educational programs, she has trained thousands of students worldwide in Reiki, holistic therapies, and intuitive development.

Her passion is to bring ancient wisdom into practical, modern tools that anyone can use for healing and self-discovery. She has authored more than forty books, ranging from the *Reiki*

Wisdom series and *Secrets of a Healer* guides to spiritual fiction exploring the Nine Spiritual Gifts. Her teaching blends Eastern philosophies, Western natural medicine, and modern energy science — always with compassion at the center.

Dr. Santego's mission is to help people connect with their inner wisdom, awaken their intuitive gifts, and live with greater balance, joy, and love. When she is not writing or teaching, she enjoys life in British Columbia, surrounded by nature's beauty, which continues to inspire her work.

ALSO AVAILABLE

For additional information on

Constance Santego's

wide range of Motivational Products, Coaching Sessions,
Spiritual Retreats,
Live Events and Educational Programs

Go to

www.ConstanceSantego.ca

Follow on Instagram - Constance_Santego and
Facebook - constancesantegoo

Subscribe and receive Free Information and Meditations on her
YouTube Channel - Constance Santego

Secrets of a Healer, Magic of Reiki

ISBN: 978-1-7772220-0-0

Secrets of a Healer, The Reiki Master's Manual

ISBN: 978-1-990062-34-6